# Curricula for Stude
# with Severe Disabil....

Students with severe disabilities comprise 2 percent of the population of learners who are impacted by intellectual, communicative, social, emotional, physical, sensory and medical issues. Increasingly, however, teachers are required to meet the challenges of creating a pedagogical balance between an individual student's strengths, needs and preferences, and core academic curricula. The need to embrace the current initiative of curriculum state standards in the debate of curricula relevance, breadth, balance and depth for students with severe disabilities is not just timely— it contributes to the evolving debate of what constitutes an appropriate curriculum for severely disabled learners.

*Curricula for Students with Severe Disabilities* supports the development of greater understandings of the role that state curriculum standards play in the pedagogical decision-making for students with severe intellectual disabilities. The book first discusses the nature and needs of these students, the curriculum for this group of learners and the recent contributions of state curriculum standards, before presenting narratives of real classrooms, teachers and students who have meaningfully integrated state curriculum standards at the kindergarten, elementary and high school levels.

**Phyllis Jones** is a Professor in the Department of Special Education at the University of South Florida, USA.

# Curricula for Students with Severe Disabilities

## Narratives of Standards-Referenced Good Practice

Phyllis Jones

Routledge
Taylor & Francis Group

NEW YORK AND LONDON

First published 2017
by Routledge
711 Third Avenue, New York, NY 10017

and by Routledge
2 Park Square, Milton Park, Abingdon, Oxon, OX14 4RN

*Routledge is an imprint of the Taylor & Francis Group, an informa business*

© 2017 Taylor & Francis

The right of Phyllis Jones to be identified as author of this work has been asserted by her in accordance with sections 77 and 78 of the Copyright, Designs and Patents Act 1988.

*Library of Congress Cataloging in Publication Data*
Names: Jones, Phyllis, author.
Title: Curricula for students with severe disabilities : narratives of standards-referenced good practice / Phyllis Jones.
Description: New York : Routledge, 2017.
Identifiers: LCCN 2016035118 | ISBN 9781138811911 (hardback) | ISBN 9781138811928 (paperback) | ISBN 9781315749112 (ebook)
Subjects: LCSH: Special education--Curricula. | Students with disabilities--Education.
Classification: LCC LC3965 .J57 2017 | DDC 371.9--dc23
LC record available at https://lccn.loc.gov/2016035118

ISBN: 978-1-138-81191-1 (hbk)
ISBN: 978-1-138-81192-8 (pbk)
ISBN: 978-1-315-74911-2 (ebk)

Typeset in Sabon
by Saxon Graphics Ltd, Derby

This book is dedicated to all teachers who enthusiastically ensure that their students with severe disabilities engage in enhanced curricular learning that also meets their personalized learning profiles. Kudos to you!

# Contents

# Acknowledgements

This book has been written despite the personal and medical issues that presented themselves. Thank you to Daniel Schwartz and Alex Masulis for your patience, support and encouragement. Two of my wonderful doctoral students, Lora Reese and Catherine Wilcox, made themselves available to support me at every opportunity. I am thankful to you both. Thank you to the teachers and administrators who collaborated with me for the narrative chapters. Your belief in my vision for the book is wonderful and I hope you are proud of the final product. Lastly, thank you to Bill Stapleton whom I always knew was my "right hand" guy but literally became my right hand when mine was broken. I appreciate everything!

# Section I

This book explores the pedagogical challenge of developing appropriate, meaningful and enriching teaching and learning for learners with severe disabilities. It is not a book about setting, where the learning takes place, but rather a book about curricular opportunities wherever the student may be. Least Restrictive Environment (LRE) is explored and supported. The learners at the center of this book should have opportunities to be in the least restrictive environment possible from the perspective of setting and context of learning. This book is not about that discourse but rather about the least restrictive environment in relation to curricula. The book explores the role of a standards-referenced curriculum in developing enriched curricular opportunities. In order to develop appropriate, meaningful and enriching teaching and learning, teachers need to have a depth of knowledge that relates to individual student learning and also a depth of knowledge about the academic curriculum.

Section I of the book is concerned with how understanding the learning profile of students is fundamental to mediate learning successfully. Chapter 1 gives an overview of the changing landscape of teaching for this group of learners. It explores some of the current issues that are pertinent to the profession. Chapter 2 focuses on the students. This involves an appreciation of the development of communicative, intellectual and related issues. The need to focus upon the learning preferences, strengths and needs of the learner are stressed. In relation to this, a teaching tool, The Engagement Profile and Scale, is presented as one way to emphasize student strengths and preferences. Chapter 3 extends the discussion of the professional landscape by exploring the pedagogical considerations that may help students with severe disabilities be successful. Research on successful pedagogy is central to this chapter. Establishing a thorough grasp of academic curriculum standards is also crucial, and this is discussed in Chapter 4. The book makes the distinction between *standards-referenced* and *standards-based* curriculum. *Standards-referenced* curriculum means that what gets taught or tested is "referenced" to or derived from learning standards (i.e., standards are the source of the content and skills taught to students—the original "reference" for the lesson). In a *standards-based* system, teaching and testing are guided by standards, and teachers work to ensure that students actually learn and are assessed on the expected age-based standards material as they progress in their education.

Section I of the book sets the context for Section II, which offers narratives of classrooms that use academic curriculum standards to develop enriched and appropriate learning opportunities for students with severe disabilities. These examples are included to give readers insights into application to practice. They are not meant to suggest a specific way a teacher should teach a student with severe disabilities, for as soon as we do this we become too prescriptive and this does not serve us, or our students, well. In Section I the term "teacher" is adopted to represent all educators who may engage in teaching students with severe disabilities. These include parents, other professionals and therapists, paraprofessionals, teaching assistants and, of course, classroom teachers. Section II uses the terms adopted by the schools to reflect the practice of the school more accurately.

# Chapter 1

# The Changing Landscape of Teaching

## What Are the Issues?

This chapter sets the context for the current work of teachers of learners with severe disabilities by discussing the following issues:

- The historical legacy of the deficit/medical model of disability.
- Embracing the Least Dangerous Assumption and Presumed Competence.
- The move towards a Least Restrictive Environment and greater inclusive learning opportunities.

These are only some of the current issues, but they serve to illustrate the sociopolitical contexts that impact teachers of learners with severe disabilities. However, before moving on, a discussion of the nature of severe disabilities will help to create a shared focus for our subsequent discourse.

### The Historical Legacy

Meet Sam:

*Sam is a 6-year-old boy diagnosed with Autism Spectrum Disorder (ASD) and Speech or Language Impairment (SLI). He has an amazing smile, enormous dimples and an infectious giggle. He has terrific eye contact, but when this occurs there is an impression that he is not looking at the adult to communicate but seems to simply enjoy eyes, and it is as though he is inspecting eyes rather than connecting for communication. Sam's favorite thing to do is dangle an object in front of his face. He dangles EVERYTHING: from string and ribbon to the broccoli on his lunch tray. He watches the movement of the dangling item, and appears completely mesmerized. He loves water, and watching it flow over his hands, and he loves long pieces of paper towel, which he rolls up and tears in strands so he can dangle them in front of his eyes. He also loves to jump on a trampoline or the floor.*

*He makes noises with his cheek and tongue. When these sounds are echoed back to him he smiles and laughs. Sam displays no verbal communication and shows no interest in pictures, even pictures of his most desired items. He will let an adult take his hand to point at a picture to get a reinforcer, but he does not extend his finger to point. He is able to choose between two desired and familiar objects, but if two pictures of the objects are held out, he will simply sit and smile, looking at the eyes of the adult. All tasks are done hand-over-hand. He shows no interest in puzzles or games, but allows pieces to be put into his hands. However, as soon as the adult lets go of a piece, he dangles it. He lets the adult take his hand and put the piece into the puzzle but he does not repeat any action independently.*

*Sam has episodes where he struggles with self-injurious behaviors. At different times of day, or sometimes for entire days, entire weeks or even months, Sam will scream and cry while hitting himself on his head, chin, neck and/or nose. There is no way to tell what is bothering him, but clearly something is very wrong. His parents have taken him to dentists, neurologists, urologists and psychologists and they have had every scan, test and procedure done to try to understand what may be happening to Sam during these highly distressed times. They have also tried medications and therapies. During these bouts, Sam barely eats and is clearly not able to attend to anything else. His longest episode of agitation and distress was 5 months. Not a day went by during that time when he was not geared up with a helmet, arm braces, gloves and, at times, even shin guards or hockey pads on his legs to prevent injury. Even with all the gear, if left on his own, he would lay down and bang his head or chin on the floor, wall or table. Sometimes walking helped but that did not always work. There were times when the adult just held on to him and hugged him, while he sobbed and tried to hit himself. His parents had a few hours per night when he would fall asleep, but 5 months went by with Sam unable to communicate what was wrong, or how he was feeling. As quickly as these bouts come on, they disappear. Sam goes back to being a smiley, giggly, sweet boy, jumping and dangling his strings.*

Clearly, this description of Sam does not represent all students with severe disabilities, but it illustrates the complexity of some of the learning issues that may be involved. These learners have an intensity to their issues that creates a complex learning profile. The profile of Sam may resonate with many readers as it highlights some of the massive challenges that Sam and his teachers face in the classroom. However, it also offers a glimpse into the strengths and wonderful connections that Sam does make with his environment.

There are indeed different terms used for students with severe disabilities. The term "students with significant cognitive disabilities" is one that was introduced in legislation (NCLB, 2001) when referring to students who take alternative assessments. "Significant cognitive disability" is not a disability category in IDEA (2004). The terms "intellectual disability" and "autism" *are* found. Sometimes the broader term "developmental disabilities" is used to be inclusive of both ASD and intellectual disabilities. Some people use the term "severe disabilities" to refer to both moderate and severe developmental disabilities. This is often captured in the eligibility category "multiple disabilities." The term "low functioning" is also used, which has obvious derogatory connotations. These are all labels, which often have negativity attached to them. Unfortunately, we work in a system that requires labels in order to access funding and resources. TASH (formerly The Association for Persons with Severe Handicaps) is a professional organization that advocates for inclusion and human rights for individuals with severe disabilities. Meyer, Peck and Brown (1991, p. 19) reprinted the TASH position statement on people with severe disabilities, stating that they: "Require extensive ongoing support in more than one major life activity ... [this] support may be required for life activities such as mobility, communication, self-care, and learning." This book adopts the term "severe" but uses other terms (e.g., "significant") when referencing research that uses such terms.

The nature of the complexity of learning needs presented by students with severe disabilities is multi-dimensional and in reality may not be captured in a formal eligibility diagnosis. Returning to Sam, the description reveals a range of discrete and interconnected issues. Sam's IEP has his primary disability as autism and secondary disability as speech and language impairment. However, when we read about Sam, we read about a boy with significant and pronounced emotional issues that would make him equally eligible for an IDEA (2004) diagnosis of emotional disturbance. In reality, the educational team recognizes the nuanced nature of Sam's learning profile and offers a responsive teaching and learning context for him. In this case, the additional resources that may be needed, for example, mental health support, hydrotherapy (water therapy) or hippotherapy (horse riding therapy), depend on the decisions of the IEP team. This could be particularly problematic where resources are scarce and when the additional learning issues are subtle.

Another dimension of the nature of the complexity of the learning needs relates to the intensity of the issues and how this intensity may vary monthly, weekly, daily and even hourly. IDEA (2004) affords value to the concept of an adverse effect of a disability on a student's educational performance. For example, a child with a visual impairment who wears correctional glasses is a great example of an appropriate support that prevents the visual impairment adversely affecting the child's educational performance. Although this example illustrates the power of an appropriate support to reduce a possible adverse effect on educational performance, it is very simple. If only all learning differences could be supported with a simple and easily accessible support! For many learners with more complicated and interrelated learning issues, the matching of supports is a much more complex process.

The IEP must include certain information about the child and the educational program designed to meet his or her unique needs. This information covers topics such as current performance, annual goals, special education and related services, accommodations, participation in state and district wide tests, needed transition services and measured progress. However, learning issues may present as more intermittent and the issues become more difficult to understand, document and capture through the IEP process. Teachers of children with severe and complex learning issues are required to be knowledgeable, thoughtful and intentional pedagogical decision makers who have a fundamental understanding of the supports that learners with severe and complex learning issues need in order to enhance their educational performance.

## The Historical Legacy of the Deficit/Medical Model of Disability

Generally, the disability category-based support provision that is the historical legacy of special education is problematic. A disability is identified and systems are built around particular disability types (often resulting in discrete provision for particular disabilities—other classrooms where children with InD, ASD or varying exceptionalities are all in separate, distinct spaces). Service provision may also be built around the levels of support children are deemed to require, resulting in support for children with extensive needs, either in separate classrooms or as a push in, pull out provision or graduated school level systems of support for learners in general education classrooms. In the USA the tradition of special education service provision specifically relates to disability categories. The reauthorization of IDEA (2004) sets out the current eligibility categories for special education service provision. However, many students with severe disabilities may still demonstrate a range of issues across categories even though they have a primary disability category label that does not include multiple disabilities. This categorization based on disability reflects a deficit medical model of disability. We have come to understand the detrimental impact and ensuing stigma to which such labeling can lead (Ho, 2004). When we spend time with students with severe disabilities we appreciate that their learning needs, preferences and strengths transcend a deficit driven label and call for a different lens to be adopted when trying to appreciate their learning profiles.

## Embracing the Least Dangerous Assumption and Presumed Competence

In 1984, Anne Donnellan, a special education researcher, wrote the criterion of least dangerous assumption: "In the absence of conclusive data, educational decisions ought to be based on assumptions which, if incorrect, will have the least dangerous effect on the likelihood that students will be able to function independently as adults" (p. 149).

It was Cheryl Jorgensen who advanced the idea of Least Dangerous Assumption by challenging historical understandings that surround disability (Jorgensen, 2006). She brought to attention that, from the outset, intelligence testing has been deemed a foundational tenet of disability. This tenet was built on the belief that intelligence can be measured in a reliable way and that low levels of intelligence, as represented in an intelligence test, earn a label of intellectual disability. Indeed, she argued that this led to the belief that learners who are labeled with an intellectual disability are not able to learn very much from general education content and the benefits of attending general education are limited. Thinking back to Sam, the process of assessing his intellectual profile is so complex that it defies a traditional intelligence test; the futility of taking him through such a test is remarkably clear. Jorgensen reminds us that, unfortunately, the history of schooling has revealed that, when we are not sure that students know, understand, can learn or have something to say (as with students with severe disabilities), we presume that they do not, cannot and probably never will. This is indeed a very dangerous assumption and leads to low expectations for students with severe disabilities. We slip into a spiral of beliefs that result in segregated schooling, or limited curricular opportunities, that do not focus on literacy or content learning. This is not because we (and by "we" I mean the teaching profession) have not got the best interests of the learners at heart, but because we are confined by the formal deficit-based ways of knowing that have formed our professional structures and systems.

Baglieri and Knopf (2004) remind us that society accepts the idea of "impairment" as "difference" and this difference is then perceived as a negative. The difference is something that diverges from an idea of an accepted norm and the person who has this difference is perceived as someone in need of being changed. This change is in the direction of the accepted idea of what is "normal." The predominance of trying to move children towards an arbitrary "normal" is referred to in the literature as the normalizing discourse. As a result of the importance attributed to the idea of something "normal," a major disservice is done to students with severe disabilities, their families and their teachers. Baglieri and Knopf (2004) point to the social structures that are developed across society based on the idea of everyone fitting the perceived view of "normal," and that these social structures create barriers to access for individuals with differences and frequently prohibit active participation in the communities in which they reside. From the perspective of teaching and schooling, these students are immediately identified as something less than the ideal norm and emphasis is placed on trying to move them, however gently and positively, to a more acceptable form of "normal." This may be to the actual detriment of the student's experience in school. The story below of Narim may help to explain this better.

*Narim is a 13-year-old boy with severe disabilities attending a center school. He is eager to communicate even though he is an emerging formal communicator. He is developing a symbolic repertoire. He loves Transformers, swimming, rebound therapy (trampoline) and hippotherapy (horse riding). He has major physical issues and uses an electric wheelchair. When in a quiet setting he is able to manipulate objects using a palmer (whole hand) grasp. Throughout the day Narim is positioned in various standing and sitting frames. I visited the classroom on a Monday morning to find Narim in a standing frame, screaming at full volume. The screaming continued and no one in the class was able to hear each other, hence there was a lot of shouting! I asked about the situation and was told by his teacher that Narim was always like this on Mondays. He started screaming when he was placed in the standing frame on a Monday morning and continued until his position was changed after an hour. He was then exhausted and slept for another hour, waking up just before lunch. The teacher explained that at home Narim spent the weekend on the floor when not in his electric wheelchair. I asked why he was placed in the standing frame and was told it was important for him to stand. I asked why it was important for him to stand and the teacher said she had been told this by the physical therapist. I was clearly somewhat confused and the teacher tried to explain that although she appreciated Narim would never walk, medically he needed to stand to support a normal flow of drainage through his body.*

I was very perplexed by this encounter with Narim. As an outside observer I did not understand all of Narim's issues and there may have been a compelling reason why this teenager needed to spend every Monday morning in such a stressful situation. However, I had to question losing one tenth of teaching time each week on a positioning issue. Narim enjoyed other physical activities, such as swimming, trampoline and horse riding, that must to some extent fulfill some of the physical needs the standing frame met. Then I returned to my first year's teaching and recalled how I had positioned and repositioned the young people in my class. I positioned the students in standing frames, in hard wooden seats, over wedges and in lying frames. None of my young students protested to the extent that Narim had done but they often shared that they were unhappy. Why had I done it? I had accepted without question that this was what the students needed: to lie, sit and stand in a somewhat normal position. I urge teachers to ask questions and try to better understand some of the professional decisions that are made about students with severe disabilities: to consider where they are happiest and see if there is any intersection between professional goals and these times.

Biklen and Burke (2006) advanced the concept of "presuming competence" (p. 166). To presume competence is to avoid assigning deficit thoughts/beliefs to the responses and behavior of a learner with severe disabilities and accept the responses and behavior as reasonable in the context of the experience of the person. Biklen and Burke asked teachers to connect with the humanity of the person with an intellectual disability and seek to understand responses and behavior empathetically from the perspective of the student.

## The Move Towards a Least Restrictive Environment

In 1975 the federal government passed the Education for all Handicapped Children Act. This law protected the rights of children with disabilities with the FAPE (Free and Appropriate Education) entitlement for every child and stated that schools should provide education to all in the least restrictive environment. This meant that, if a special needs child could be educated in the general classroom, schools had to provide the resources for this to occur. The legislation was renamed Individuals with Disabilities Education Act (IDEA, 1997; 2004) and was the legislation that stated that all students should have access to general curriculum content. No Child Left Behind (NCLB, 2001) required that all students be assessed on state standards, but alternative assessments could be used for students with significant cognitive disabilities who could not participate in the state assessment. The educational rights of students with disabilities are also ensured by two other federal laws: Section 504 of the Rehabilitation Act (Amendment of 1995) and the 1990 Americans with Disabilities Act (ADA). The Elementary and Secondary Education Act (ESEA, 2010) reauthorization proposal increased support for the inclusion and improved outcomes of students with disabilities. The Regular Education Initiative (REI), introduced in 1986 by former Assistant Secretary of Education, Madeleine C. Will, called for general educators to become more responsible for the schooling of learners who have special needs in their school. Through this initiative, Secretary Will questioned the distinct system of special education (Harkins, 2012). We can see that special education reform policies and practice have developed under the guidance of federal mandate for students with disabilities "to be educated to the maximum extent appropriate with peers without disabilities" (Yell, 2006, p. 310). It began with "mainstreaming" in the 1970s, shifted to "integration" during the 1980s, and currently focuses on the "inclusion" of students with a particular emphasis on access to core academic general curriculum content rather than on placement *per se* (Turnbull, Wehmeyer, & Shogren, 2010).

## Conclusion

This chapter has sketched out the landscape of key issues that form the context in which teachers of learners with severe disabilities teach in schools. It began by discussing the nature of severe disabilities through the story of Sam and confirmed the problems that arise with deficit and categorical perspectives. This developed into a discussion of the historical legacy of the deficit/medical model of disability and the need to embrace the concepts of Least Dangerous Assumption and Presumed Competence. The chapter ended by highlighting the move towards a Least Restrictive Environment and greater inclusive learning opportunities. The discussion of these issues is intended to illustrate the evolving school contexts in which teachers of this group of learners are working. It is the teacher's professional role to ensure learners receive meaningful and enriching learning opportunities. Striking the pedagogical balance between individual student needs, strengths and preferences and the demands of a standards-referenced curriculum is a highly tuned professional skill: a skill that requires teachers to be extremely knowledgeable, not only in the highly personalized learning profiles that students with severe disabilities present, but also highly knowledgeable in curriculum standards. I believe teachers cannot mediate learning without these two sets of knowledge and this book intends to support the building of both. The focus of the book is curriculum and pedagogy; there is a whole additional discourse associated with assessment and testing. While the book will refer to assessment in relation to assessment for teaching and learning, it will not analyze in depth the sociopolitical issues of accountability and high stakes testing.

# Chapter 2

# Building Understandings of Students

This chapter explores some ways that teachers can better understand the learning needs of students with severe disabilities. However, it is important to remember that the learners we discuss, the learners we teach in the classroom, the learners who present with incredibly complex learning profiles, are learners who are children and young people first. They have the fundamental needs that all children and young people have: the need to be valued, be respected, to have fun, be loved and be recognized as active learners. As teachers we get caught up in the detail of managing learner needs and, very often, their challenging behavior. Sometimes we may need a reminder about the joy and fun that is a central human need. The importance of developing and building relationships with our students is fundamental. I think across my career this is an area that stands out as crucial to the work I have carried out in schools.

The chapter examines some of the understandings we have relating to the personalized learning profiles that learners may present. We spend time discussing communicative and intellectual development that offers a foundation for understanding learners with severe disabilities. However, we know that many of these learners present a myriad of learning issues. This chapter focuses upon the central issues of communication and intellectual development, but we also briefly discuss medical, social, mental health and sensory issues. These additional issues may have a powerful influence on how a learner is able and ready to participate in learning. The challenge is to make sense of personalized learning profiles as we present learners with standards-referenced curriculum opportunities. When this occurs, meaningful participation is more likely to ensue.

No matter how complex a student's personalized learning profile is, a focus upon engagement in learning needs to be a priority. An assessment tool, The Engagement Profile (Carpenter et al., 2011), is introduced as a way that teaching teams can build additional understandings about a student's engagement in learning. This additional understanding of personal learning profiles contributes to building greater appreciation of student participation with enhanced curricular opportunities. The chapter ends with a discussion of the role of personalized learning profiles that embrace learners' needs, strengths, interests and preferences.

## Understandings of Development

To begin with, a word of warning. Currently, our understanding of how communication and intellect develop is influenced by developmental psychology. We have a strong body of research, which analyses the development of communication and intellect in learners who are typically developing. It is important that we hold a strong grasp of this research so that we have an understanding about phases and critical stages of development. However, our understanding of how learners with severe disabilities learn tells us that their development may often be "spikey" and not follow what we understand to be the usual path. We may be guided by theories and stages of development in learners who are typically developing, but we should not be bound by them. They may, or may not, serve the learners we are working with well and may actually encourage a deficit view of students' abilities. We need to be particular and thoughtful about how we view learners through the lens of developmental psychology. If the lens contributes to our constructive understanding of how learners are interacting, engaging and making sense of their environment, then it earns its place in our repertoire of understandings. If it only serves to show the learner in a negative way, we may need to explore other ways to understand them. Such a way, for example, might be dynamic assessment.

### Communication Issues

Communication is at the heart of living in a social world. Without shared communication, life can be confusing and very lonely. Many children with severe disabilities also have significant issues with communication. Returning to Sam, we read that his communication is not always shared with adults and in some situations his behavior becomes his most powerful form of communication: giggling, he is happy, connecting to his own sounds being echoed back to him with smiles; screaming and hitting himself in times of distress. Talk to any teacher of students with severe disabilities and they will tell you that developing shared communication is a top priority in pedagogical decision-making. Understanding that communication is a joint effort that involves the coordination of responses between two or more people (Bunning, 2009) accepts how complex the process of communication is. The National Center and State Collaborative (NCSC), a project led by 5 centers and 24 states, has developed curricular and instructional resources for teachers related to their enactment of state standards in classrooms for students with severe disabilities (NCSC, 2015). In appreciation of the crucial role of communication, NCSC collaborated with the American Speech-Language-Hearing Association (ASHA) to create a professional development Communication Toolkit to support teachers when teaching students whose learning profiles demand focus on the development of communication. The toolkit will be examined in more detail in Chapter 4.

Teachers of students with severe disabilities have shared that the development of communication is a priority in their pedagogical decision-making (Jones & Lawson, 2015). Communication can either empower or disempower learners with severe disabilities. To enable a learner to communicate with others is to give them a way to meet their physical, social and intellectual needs as social human beings. Communication can be understood as the communicative engagement that is received, comprehended and also expressed and shared. An idea of the milestones children may generally pass through offers a teacher a framework of understanding communication that may be helpful in pedagogical decision-making. As with intellectual development, there is an historical preponderance with communication scales and assessments based on early typical childhood development. Goldbart and Ware (2015) offer a very good general overview of what communication is and how it develops. Teachers of learners with severe disabilities benefit from an appreciation of the typical development of communication, understanding that their students with severe disabilities may present a different communicative development profile. The learners may also present different levels in how they receive communication (referred to as "receptive") and how they express communication (referred to as "expressive"). Communicative intent applies to both receptive and expressive communication and often presents a challenge to many teachers of students with severe disabilities as they ascertain, appreciate and participate in intentional communication with their students. Table 2.1 illustrates some of the major receptive and expressive communication milestones that may typically develop across the first 3 years. This is a general overview to give an idea of the range of communicative skills that typically develop.

Speech and language therapists have expertise and in-depth understanding of communication development, communication delay and communication disorders. Communication is their life and they have much expertise to offer in understanding communication and strategies to nurture meaningful communication. The research of Vandereet et al. (2010) shows that students with severe learning issues employ a dominance of communicative behaviors that are classified as requesting interactions ("Can I have...," "I want...") rather than communicative interactions that point out or share something interesting ("This is interesting," "Look at this..."). This may reflect the individual profile of communicative development of the student or it may reflect the opportunities for

*Table 2.1* Major Receptive and Expressive Typical Communication Milestones

| | Receptive Communication | Expressive Communication |
|---|---|---|
| *Typically develops across the first year* | Startles to loud sounds.<br><br>Smiles when spoken to.<br><br>Moves eyes in direction of sounds and responds to changes in tone of voice.<br><br>Notices toys that make sounds.<br><br>Enjoys games like peek-a-boo and pat-a-cake.<br><br>Recognizes words for common items like "cup," "shoe," "book" or "juice."<br><br>Begins to respond to requests (e.g., "Come here," or "Want more?"). | Makes pleasure sounds (cooing).<br><br>Cries differently for different needs.<br><br>Smiles at others.<br><br>Vocalizes excitement and displeasure.<br><br>Uses gestures to communicate (waving, holding arms to be picked up).<br><br>Imitates different speech sounds.<br><br>Has one or two words (hi, dog, dada, mama) around first birthday, although sounds may not be clear. |
| *Typically develops across the second year* | Points to named pictures in book.<br><br>Points to a few body parts when asked (nose, eyes, tummy).<br><br>Consistently follows simple requests ("Push the bus!").<br><br>Responds to simple questions ("Where's the dog?" "What's in your bag?").<br><br>Likes listening to simple stories—may want the same story, rhyme or game repeated many times.<br><br>Enjoys singing songs or saying simple rhymes. | Vocabulary repertoire steadily increases.<br><br>Asks two-word questions ("Where ball?" "What's that?").<br><br>Combines two words to make simple sentences ("Dog go," "More cake").<br><br>Words becoming clearer as more initial consonants are used. |
| *Typically develops across the third year* | Responds to two-stage commands ("Get the car and put it in the box").<br><br>Responds to requests about contrasting concepts or meanings ("Show me hot/cold; in/on").<br><br>Notices purposeful sounds like the telephone or doorbell, may point, become excited, get adults' attention, or respond themselves. | Vocabulary is exploding!<br><br>Utterances are usually one, two or three words long.<br><br>Asks for things with two-part component request that may be accompanied by gesture ("Teddy book," "Bus song").<br><br>Draws attention to something by naming it ("Cow") or one of its attributes ("Brown!") or by commenting ("Wow!"). |

communication we develop for students with severe disabilities. The work of Grove and colleagues (Grove et al., 2015) shows how enriched literacy opportunities can nurture communicative interactions that share interests or experiences.

It is also vital, when considering communication issues, that the role of behavior is understood. Everyone communicates through behavior during every moment in every day, even if unintentionally. We may cry when sad, or yawn when bored or tired. Children engage in challenging behavior for a reason. A child who displays challenging behavior is communicating something. The purpose of the behavior may be to get someone's attention, stop a non-preferred activity or meet personal sensory needs. Some behavior may appear destructive, but the child may crave the physical sensation of the destructive behavior (for example, tearing paper or eating clothes). Sometimes children may lose control so their behavior is very inappropriate (for example, kicking or hitting out). Understanding behavior as communication requires accepting that there is always a reason behind it. A challenge to teachers is to find out the meaning behind behavior and offer consistent, reliable, caring support and guidance, especially during difficult times. Teachers need to understand the function of the behavior (what it is communicating) prior to implementing any teaching interventions. Functional Behavior Assessments (FBAs) do just this through the forum of a multi-professional assessment. I learned the value of considering the communicative intent of behavior early in my teaching career.

*I was teaching a 6th Grade class of nine students with severe disabilities. I worked intensively with a boy with Fragile X syndrome, particularly related to challenging behavior. When he first came into the class he engaged in a lot of hitting out behavior with adults and peers alike. Over the first few weeks I developed a behavior modification plan. The student and I enjoyed a strong relationship and he responded well to the plan. Over a month the behavior reduced significantly. As you can imagine, I was very happy with myself! But, to my dismay, my student pretty quickly began pulling hair; his hair, adult hair and the hair of his peers. I was a tenacious young teacher and, putting my dismay to one side, I created another behavior modification plan, to which my student responded very positively. This cycle continued for about 8 months: the student displaying particular behavior, which was modified through a behavior plan, only to be replaced by an equally challenging but different behavior. I was perplexed and asked the visiting school educational psychologist to come into class. It was decided we would video the young boy across the week and view the video as a team, which included mum, the classroom team, deputy head teacher and educational psychologist. When we watched the video we realized that the young boy was visually referencing the school bell that was located above one of the doors. In England the school day is always structured around the school bell. There is a bell for assembly, a bell for play time, a bell for lesson change, a bell for lunch and a bell for home time. Indeed, across the school day there are a whole lot of school bell ringing times. We wondered if the bell was in some way causing distress or triggering the behavior. We were 8 months into the school year and did not want to spend time collecting data about the bell and behavior as we already had our hypothesis. We implemented a program in which we first explained to the student this is what we were thinking and for a week we would make sure he was out of the room before the bell rang at any time. During the second week we introduced headphones and offered these to the student a minute before the bell rang, each and every time the bell was scheduled to ring. The behavior of the young boy improved. He used the headphones for the rest of the school year and his behavior was much calmer without the yo-yoing we had experienced earlier in the year.*

I tell this story to emphasize how important it is to not only understand the communicative function of behavior but also how difficult a process this is. My student was telling me, "I hate the bell sound," "The bell hurts my ears," "The bell frightens me." It took me a while to hear this message from him. Indeed, it took a multi-professional collaborative to help me, his classroom teacher, gain more accurate insights about the behavior.

### Intellectual Issues

How a student understands and makes sense of the world comprises the intellectual area of development. This is often also referred to as cognitive development. Learners with severe disabilities definitely demonstrate issues with how they understand and make sense of the world around them and this tends to be a central focus of teaching and learning. A major concern relates to the tools professionals use to assess intellectual ability. First, in diagnosis, IQ tests remain a central indicator of intelligence for students with severe disabilities and also a gate keeper for eligibility to IDEA disability categories, (e.g., Intellectual Disability). These are tests that determine issues with:

- Conceptual skills—language and literacy; money, time and number concepts; and self-direction.
- Social skills—interpersonal skills, social responsibility, self-esteem, gullibility, naivety (i.e., wariness), social problem solving and the ability to follow rules, obey laws and avoid being victimized.
- Practical skills—activities of daily living (personal care), occupational skills, healthcare, travel/transportation, schedules/routines, safety, use of money and use of the telephone.

More usually than not, the tests do not serve the students or the teachers well. A story shared by a parent about her son with Down syndrome illustrates this:

*Jack was 8 years old and had experienced a very nurturing and positive time being included with his peers in a local general education classroom. It was time for his reassessment for eligibility for services under the category of intellectual disability. Jack also had a recurrent and life-threatening heart issue and his current intellectual disability eligibility enabled him to qualify for a medical waiver and receive the medical support needed for his health issues. Jack's dad was self-employed in a construction business, which was struggling to survive in the recession. Jack's mom was a qualified teacher, but not working at the time. In the new IQ test Jack did very well and increased his score by 4 points. However, the new score prevented Jack from qualifying for a medical waiver and therefore made access to important health services much more difficult.*

This was a real sting in the tail of the wonderful progress that Jack had made and highlights how IQ tests are very problematic for this group of learners. IQ tests may also serve to indicate a general level of intellectual response to the "cognitive" context of the test but may not represent how a student actually understands and makes meaning of the world. How one gains insight into this is probably one of the six million dollar questions in education. The problems associated with IQ testing may not affect professionals, who appreciate the issues and, therefore, do not allow IQ test results to play a significant role in their deliberations and instructional decisions. However, when IQ scores are associated with resources it becomes problematic indeed. Second, there are struggles associated with some of the tools used to understand the level of intellectual functioning for instructional purposes and measuring how a student responds to the teaching and learning. Many developmental psychology assessment scales that have been historically adopted are also based on babies or young children and assume children learn in a regular, linear and hierarchical way. A story from my own teaching helps to shed light on some of the problems:

*As a newly qualified teacher I found myself teaching a group of 16 to 19-year-old students with profound and multiple learning disabilities. The young people were coming to the end of their school careers constantly being assessed using development scales that reflect the first stage of Piaget's intellectual development—the sensory motor stage. As a new teacher I did exactly the same! I assessed each of my students using the Uzgiris and Hunt Infant Development Assessment Scale (Uzgiris & Hunt, 1975). The scale has discrete sections that relate to understandings that objects have permanence even when they disappear, understandings that actions create reactions, understandings that particular actions receive particular adult attention (both positive and negative) and understandings that symbols represent objects or actions in the world. My students seemed to like me and responded well to the assessment activities I presented to them. There were varied responses to each of the discrete areas by all the students, except one. This was the section that represents understandings that particular actions receive particular adult attention. All my students scored their highest scores in this section. I realized that I was engaged with a group of young people who were living life and bringing a wealth of experiences, interacting with key people, enjoying being with them and learning to have their needs met through their interaction with others. They had a lot of lived experiences they were building on that this assessment happened to capture. But the Assessment Scale did not manage to capture other aspects of their intellectual engagement that I increasingly came to believe they had through my anecdotal life experiences with them. As the weeks and months passed the general areas of the early development scale influenced my understandings of the young people, but the scale as an assessment tool was relegated to the file cabinet in the corner of the room. My challenge was to try to understand how each young person was showing understandings that objects have permanence even when they disappear (understandings that actions create reactions), understandings that symbols represent objects or actions in the world and more sophisticated understandings that particular actions receive particular adult attention (both positive and negative).*

This story is shared to show teachers that learners with severe disabilities have capacities that we, sometimes for a brief moment, get a glimpse of, but for a lot of the time, do not. It is shared as an important lesson to continue to search for ways to understand students who present with severe disabilities. Being cognizant of the wealth of literature on child development is important to offer a context for understanding students' interaction with people and their environment. The typical flow of child development is represented in stages or phases. Piaget's developmental psychology schemas (Jean Piaget Archives Foundation, 1989) set out four stages, represented as Sensory Motor, Pre-operational, Concrete Operational and Formal Operations. In each of these stages children develop essential skills that move them from pre-symbolic to abstract thinkers. Teachers benefit from an appreciation of this typical flow of skills development, but must remember that students with severe disabilities may portray an uneven profile of development and their journey from pre-symbolic thinkers, through to abstract thinkers, may be different. Indeed, developmental psychologists who have replicated Piaget's experiments have shown that there is much variance across children who are typically developing (Gopnik et al., 2001). Table 2.2 sets out the general areas of typical skill development on the journey from pre-symbolic to abstract thinkers. However, remember that some students with severe disabilities may not follow a linear path and it is important for us to present learning that is in the zone of proximal development (Gopnik et al., 2001). That is, development that is in the higher range of student learning.

*Table 2.2* Piaget's Stages of Intellectual Development

| Symbolic Area of Growth | Brief Overview |
|---|---|
| Pre- and early symbolic thinking | Key understandings emerging through this phase are the development of mental representations or ideas about something. During this phase understandings are only from the child's point of view and children are often referred to as egocentric. Object permanence develops (when something disappears it continues to exist—the foundation of memory), and understandings of cause and effect (when one thing can cause an effect on another). *(Typically associated with birth to 2 years.)* |
| Early symbolic moving into more established symbolic thinking | Key understandings emerging through this phase are built around general thought processes although children remain egocentric and maintain understandings that everything that exists has some kind of consciousness (referred to as animism). Across this phase children become more established symbolic thinkers. They develop understandings that objects can be grouped together in multiple ways, that we can correspond to objects and they correspond to each other in a one-to-one way. They recognize patterns in the environment to be able to continue them. *(Typically associated with 2 to 7 years.)* |
| Concrete symbolic thinkers | Key understandings emerging through this phase are built around thought processes that become more rational and mature. Key understandings of this phase are that objects are not what they always appear to be (referred to as conservation), and understandings that when things appear to change they actually remain the same (referred to as reversibility). During this phase, children appear less egocentric and more altruistic. *(Typically associated with 7 to 11 years.)* |
| Abstract symbolic thinkers | Key understandings emerging through this phase are built around thought processes. Key ideas associated with this stage are hypothetic deductive reasoning (reasoning begins with a hypothesis, an idea, that is then tested) and propositional reasoning (logical validity of assertions are evaluated without reference to real-world circumstances). *(Typically associated with 11 to 16 years.)* |

Many of the concepts inherent in the curriculum standards can be traced back to early symbolic thinking skills. For example, reading is one of the most sophisticated forms of understanding that symbols represent an object. However, it is important to embrace a healthy skepticism towards the traditional tools employed for assessing early intellectual/symbolic development.

### Medical Issues

Many students have co-existing medical issues that may be lifelong, temporary or sustained. These issues may have an incredible impact on the wellbeing of the student and many medications have significant side effects. It is crucial that we keep very open and continuous communication with home and the family. The impact of a missed dose of medicine can be devastating on a student's wellbeing.

### Social Issues

Many students may have issues interacting in a social environment, whether or not they have a diagnosis of Autism Spectrum Disorder (ASD). It is important that the teacher builds the teaching and learning to take into account these social interaction issues. We have learned a lot from the literature on ASD to have access to strategies that may support these children, including social stories, priming and visuals.

### Mental Health Issues

Co-occurring mental health issues have a massive impact on learners' engagement at school. We will discuss some of the more familiar ones, but a teacher may need to research the particular diagnosis of the student. Learners with Anxiety Disorder worry excessively, find it difficult to control the worry and demonstrate restlessness, fatigue, irritability or difficulty concentrating (Silverman & Field, 2011). Many of our students have Reactive Attachment Disorder and may seek or respond to comfort in bizarre ways. They may present as inexplicably irritated, sad or fearful, or are minimally socially or emotionally responsive to others. They also have particular issues with self-regulation in the school context (Schwartz & Davis, 2006). Some students have Oppositional Defiant Disorder and demonstrate a pattern of negative, hostile and defiant behavior, arguing constantly with adults. They may deliberately annoy people, defy requests or rules and often blame others for their mistakes or misbehaviors. These students often present as easily annoyed by others, or are often angry, resentful, spiteful or vindictive (Althoff et al., 2014). Learners with Obsessive Compulsive Disorder (OCD) may worry about contamination, (e.g., others sneezing or coughing, or about touching things that may be dirty) or demonstrate superstitious behaviors (such as avoiding stepping on cracks or having to follow a particular sequence of behaviors before entering a room, etc.). They may also insist that everything must be in the same order at all times. Learners may have an additional fear for safety and security, constantly checking all doors, windows, lockers or desks, and may hoard things in their locker (Chaturvedi, Murdick, & Gartin,

2014). Those with depression have difficulty concentrating, appear to forget everything and appear to "switch off" or sleep a lot (Maag, Swearer, & Toland, 2009). Learners with co-existing mental health issues are likely to be prescribed psychiatric medication (Yell et al., 2013). These include medicines classified as stimulants, antidepressants, mood stabilizers and antipsychotics. Each medicine has several side effects that may have a major impact on their learning.

### Sensory Issues

Many of our learners have additional issues with the way they make sense of their immediate surroundings. They may present as overly sensitive—known as hypersensitivity—where sights, sounds and feelings present as an assault, which may impact them very harshly. Alternatively, some appear hyposensitive, where they seem immune to sensory input and are very difficult to motivate and engage. Many of the learners may have sensory integration complications. This is where they have difficulties receiving, filtering, retrieving and making sense of environmental input. For some of them, the classroom can be a very cruel and lonely place. As special education teachers we are experienced at gathering all the individual presentations of a student's learning profile and working to make our classrooms much more sensory friendly (sights, sounds and touch).

## Engagement in Learning

Engagement in learning activities is the key factor in acquiring knowledge and skills (Iovannone et al., 2003) and so it makes sense to say that any learning is dependent on engagement. Any level of engagement in a learning activity reflects the personalized learning profile of students (Carpenter et al., 2015). Fredericks, Blumenfeld and Paris (2004) state that increases in student engagement in learning occur when an experience is meaningful to a student. However, to ensure meaningful engagement can be challenging, especially when personalized learning profiles are complex and often appear overwhelming. An Engagement Profile tool is now shared that offers a way to appreciate how children with severe disabilities (and those with profound and multiple disabilities) are making sense of, and interacting with, their environment. It may be one additional form of analysis that teachers can add to their pedagogical decision-making repertoire.

## The Engagement Profile (EP) and Engagement Scale (ES)

Emerging from a 2011 United Kingdom (UK) based research project (Carpenter et al., 2011), focused on learners with complex disabilities, came the Engagement Profile and Scale (EPS). Here is a brief overview to raise awareness of it as an assessment tool that teaching teams may adopt to analyze moments of high student engagement in learning. Preferably, a multi-disciplinary team will adopt the EPS to support the analysis of the positive ways students with complex disabilities engage with their environment. Being cognizant of the nature of how high engagement presents naturally contributes to how the team facilitates future learning opportunities. The intention of the EPS is to develop greater appreciation of elevated learner engagement through a reflection of student engagement in preferred activities. This leads to the understanding of personalized learning pathways that learners may present, upon which teaching teams can capitalize in the crafting of future learning opportunities. The EPS consists of two parts: the Engagement Profile (EP) and the Engagement Scale (ES).

### The Engagement Profile (EP)

The purpose of the profile is to analyze high engagement student behaviors as demonstrated by a student with severe disabilities. There are seven indicators that make up the EP and these are illustrated in Table 2.3, which also includes brief working definitions of the indicators. However, it is acknowledged that, for individual students, the indicators may present very differently. It is important to be aware of this variability. The list of indicators is not intended to show a hierarchy.

A professional team composed of everyone who has knowledge and regular interaction with the student collaborates to complete the EP. The

Table 2.3 Engagement Profile Indicators and Brief Definitions

| EP Indicator | Brief Definition |
| --- | --- |
| Awareness | First stage in the process of learning. The consciousness or recognition of something. |
| Curiosity | The need, thirst or desire to explore, know about or learn. |
| Investigation | A detailed or thorough inquiry or systematic examination. |
| Discovery | Something previously unknown or recognized, which is located and revealed—whether by intent or chance. |
| Anticipation | Expectation arising from foreknowledge; predicting or feeling something is about to happen. |
| Persistence | Continued effort; perseverance; determination; firmness of purpose; refusing to give up or let go. |
| Initiation | Taking the first step or setting in motion; beginning or originating an event; taking the lead. |

team may include, but is not limited to, teachers, teaching assistants, family members, speech and language therapists, occupational therapists, physical therapists and visiting itinerant specialist teachers. Through this process the team builds up understandings of learning preferences and reinforcers, crucial knowledge as future teaching and learning is planned.

### The Engagement Scale (ES)

A 4-minute video that depicts the highest engagement from the student is prepared. This represents any activity showing some level of student engagement that is self-initiated and positive. Through collaborative analysis of the video, the team notes behavior that represents the indicators of the EP. Team members rate each indicator on the rating scale shown in Table 2.4, Engagement Profile Rating Scale.

The team discusses each score and, through consensus building, an agreed overall score of engagement is established. It is at this point that the team explores possible reasons why the engagement was high or low and then decides the next steps from a pedagogical perspective. Questions that teams are encouraged to engage with are:

- What happened?
- What did not happen and why?
- What will I do next time and why?
- How will I make the activity more appealing?

Carpenter and colleagues (Carpenter et al., 2015) have also developed an Inquiry Framework to help with this phase of the Engagement Profile and Scale assessment process. The total ES score can be used as a measure of student progress over time across a range of activities. The EPS is repeated regularly (once every couple of weeks) over the course of a semester. Through the UK research project, the EPS was trialed across the UK, and in schools in Eire, America and New Zealand. There was strong agreement that the EPS positively supported detailed assessment

*Table 2.4* Engagement Profile Rating Scale

| 0 | 1 | 2 | 3 | 4 |
|---|---|---|---|---|
| No focus/ inattentive/ unresponsive. | Low and minimal levels of engagement with the activity with some evidence of awareness. | Fleeting and random/ emerging but unpredictable engagement with the activity. | Engagement with the activity for the majority of time. | Engaged fully for the full duration of the activity. |

and planning that led to increased higher levels of student engagement for students with complex learning needs (Carpenter et al., 2011).

## Conclusion

As teachers, we appreciate the need to facilitate the active engagement in learning. We do this by paying particular attention to the integration of students' strengths, interests and needs (Young, 2010). We pay attention to their intellectual and communicative strengths and needs. We pay attention to how issues of perception, physical, sensory, medical and mental health impact learning. We also pay attention to learner preferences and reinforcers. It is also suggested that it is helpful to analyze moments of highest learner engagement through the Engagement Profile and Scale. It is only when we pay attention to all of these aspects of a student's personalized learning that we can mediate successful and meaningful experiences with a standards-referenced curriculum.

# Chapter 3

# Curriculum Considerations and Pedagogical Decision-Making

## Introduction

The crucial role of multi-professional working frames this chapter and highlights the powerful contribution it makes when teaching students with severe disabilities. We consider the potential role of brain-based learning and how understanding of this may influence our potential decision-making. Key considerations of teaching and learning for this group of students are then discussed that may inform the decisions made about teaching and learning for students with severe disabilities. Readers will realize that these considerations are not relevant to this group of students alone. They are considerations that every teacher may deliberate in some shape or form. However, for students with severe disabilities, the strategies inherent in the considerations, instead of being different, may be much more explicit and have a more intense application (Lewis & Norwich, 2005). These considerations are also not distinct from each other, but blend together to create a rich tapestry of pedagogy where considerations enjoy a symbiotic relationship with each other.

## Multi-Professional Working

The term "multi-professional working" refers to how professionals collaborate together better to serve the complex needs of learners with all disabilities, but is particularly relevant for learners with severe and complex learning profiles. It involves team members sharing roles, sharing knowledge and accepting the fluid nature of each professional's role in the personalized education of students (Allday, Neilson-Gatti, & Hudson, 2013; Dahle, 2003). The impact of multi-professional working on the quality of teaching and learning for students with disabilities is established (Silverman & Field, 2011; Jacobs & Harvey, 2010). Collaboration, a fundamental skill of multi-professional working, is an effective practice for meeting complex needs of students with disabilities. However, collaboration is not a natural behavior for everyone and can be a difficult process to facilitate and in which to participate. Collaboration as a working process needs to be nurtured, planned and evaluated (Hentz & Jones, 2011).

## Brain-Based Learning

Developments in neuroscience have allowed insight into the roles that different parts of the brain have on learning and how this may be different for different groups of learners. We have become much more knowledgeable about the function of particular parts of the brain and the amazing compensatory features of the brain. Developments in Magnetic Resonance Imaging (MRI) suggest that learners with particular disabilities have different brain-mapping patterns. For example, learners with Fetal Alcohol Syndrome Disorder (FASD) have significantly compromised cerebellum and basal ganglia. We are just beginning to engage with the implications of this new knowledge but know enough to ensure our teaching and learning is informed by brain-based learning. This includes:

- Build in environmental supports (safety).
- Build in predictable routines.
- Ensure experiences are repeated and repeated again.
- Pay attention to emotions and feelings.
- Use multisensory teaching techniques.
- Use differentiated teaching techniques.

## Curriculum Considerations

The curriculum and pedagogical journeys that schools travel to provide meaningful learning opportunities for students with severe disabilities are constantly evolving. Browder, Wakeman and Flowers (2007) point out that curricular focus of the content of the curriculum has changed over time and the discourse has become quite dichotomized between functional versus academic content. No Child Left Behind (NCLB, 2002) and the Reauthorization of the Individuals with Disabilities Education Act (IDEA, 2004) both emphasize academic standards as a core part of the curriculum. This book acknowledges the existence of multiple approaches in order for readers to consider a balanced approach to pedagogical decision-making for this group of learners. The developmental curriculum, the functional life skills curriculum and the evolution of the academic curriculum are briefly discussed prior to the discussion of pedagogical issues. Pedagogical considerations, which support the development of meaningful learning opportunities in a standards-referenced curriculum for learners with severe disabilities, are shared.

### Developmental Curriculum

The developmental curriculum is founded on the premise that all children learn in the same way and through the same phases in key areas of development. This was the emphasis of my pre-service training. I became adept at using developmental assessments to find the developmental level at which my students appeared to be performing, and crafting learning opportunities to move them through the stages of development. The problem I encountered was that the students I taught with severe disabilities did not communicate or show their levels of ability in the same ways as their typically developing peers. This is demonstrated through the story of Johnny.

*Johnny was a young man (18) who was a member of my class. Johnny had severe disabilities. He was able to eye point in response to specific requests and use BIGmack switches to initiate activities and ask for more. Johnny was incredibly social and was very aware of his environment and the people within it. He loved music. He used to laugh his socks off when my husband "did an Elvis" and sang Blue Suede Shoes in front of him. He could be motivated to do many simple tasks if I was able to integrate the theme tunes of the TV soap operas that he watched with his mother. In response to the developmental assessments I was using he was performing as an emerging symbolic thinker and appeared to be at the stage where I designed activities to promote sorting, classifying or sequencing skills. However, he appeared uninterested in all my carefully planned activities and often turned away. I had an intuition that he was performing below level and he was much more able than my teaching was supporting him to show. It was frustrating for both of us. The time was the mid-1980s and the curricular landscape was developmental and functional in England at that time. I had a feeling he needed more but I did not know what that more might be. This feeling was supported one day in class when I had come across different sized white and milk chocolate buttons and used them to assess his ability to sort by two attributes. Johnny completed the sorting activity immediately and confirmed to me that he was operating at a higher conceptual level than his engagement in the classroom demonstrated.*

What the story of Johnny reminds me of is how a strong adherence to a developmental curriculum, with a principle of a child needing to show performance at one level prior to moving to the next, may not serve some of our students with severe disabilities well.

### Functional Life Skills Curriculum

The functional life skills curriculum focuses on the skills judged to be needed for the students to function in real life, their local community and vocational job opportunities. Functional life skills focus on personal independence skills and recreational skills that are intended to improve the quality of life. Browder et al. (2006) reflect that the functional life curriculum "was adopted in the absence of any other approach to impart skills to students with severe disabilities in the mid 1970s" (p. 6). Emphasis is given to the development of a range of domestic, vocational and recreational skills. A specialized learning curriculum emerged where practical skills were given high value, for example, washing clothes, simple cookery, cleaning and using local public transport. Classroom and school opportunities for these students looked different from their typically developing peers in a general education classroom. In a functional curriculum the emphasis is on functional independence. IEP goals that relate to functional routines drive curricular opportunities and students are prepared for simple tasks in the community that are related to personal independence, such as housekeeping tasks or using public transport (Ford, Davern, & Schnorr, 2001, p. 214). Functional curricula influenced decision-making at elementary, middle, high and post-school phases. This book is not suggesting that these become irrelevant in the school career of learners with severe disabilities, but rather that these students need enhanced curricular opportunities that are driven by something other than daily living skills.

## The Evolution of the Academic Curriculum

The standards-based reform and accountability movements influenced the discussion of the academic curriculum, which emphasizes access to general education in the standards curriculum content of Reading, Math, Science and Social Studies (Browder et al., 2003). The integration of an academic and functional life curriculum was suggested as a more balanced view of the curriculum for students with severe disabilities by Collins, Kleinert and Land (2006), who point out that in this curriculum "Functional academic skills include basic Math concepts, such as number recognition, counting and computations that can be applied to such skills as telling time, managing money and performing measurements" (p. 201).

This blended curricular approach allows students with severe disabilities access to general education curriculum standards while blending functional life skills throughout the school day. The blended approach enhances the independence of students with severe disabilities in both inclusive settings and adult life as well as supporting general education activities with peers (Ryndak, Jackson, & White, 2013). Browder et al. (2006) asserted that a blended approach allows teachers to focus on functional life skills and academics, and prepares students with significant cognitive disabilities for life after high school.

Teachers are being encouraged to have higher academic expectations for students with severe intellectual disabilities. Browder et al. (2009) found that higher standards ultimately led to higher expectations and outcomes for this group of students and, at the same time, improved quality of life and increased means and opportunities for self-determination. We know that students with extensive support needs are placed in general education classes less often and receive more of their supports from educational assistants than from licensed teachers (Copeland & Cosbey, 2010). Further, we also know that IEP goals that are aligned with general education outcomes help this group of learners to participate and progress in the general education curriculum, and to access the standards that their peers without disabilities are receiving (Thompson et al., 2001).

As we consider engagement with curriculum standards, teachers may want to consider how the opportunities afforded by the standards can enhance the whole life of a student with severe disabilities. The intention is enhanced access to educational, vocational and recreational activities, while addressing the limited focus of the functional life skills curriculum (Ayres et al., 2011).

## Pedagogical Considerations

Through experience and research we have gleaned some important understandings about how some learners with severe disabilities learn. Circumspection is advised, when using a term like "some," for as soon as we have a catch-all statement we will come across a learner with severe disabilities who does not match what we have come to understand about the group of learners. The considerations offered in this chapter may not apply to all learners with severe disabilities, and do not apply to any particular student all of the time, but may prove helpful to a teacher in his/her pedagogical decision-making. Browder et al. (2014) reviewed the current literature in text books and other research aimed at teacher preparation regarding teaching and learning for students with severe disabilities. This review of the literature covered "What to teach" as well as "How to teach."

### What to Teach

An overview of what emerged in the review by Browder et al. (2014) about what to teach is seen in Table 3.1, What to Teach.

It is clear from this that current literature supports the teaching of academic skills along with personalized individual skills. In the consideration of how to teach, both academic and personalized skills are covered.

*Table 3.1* What to Teach

| | |
|---|---|
| *Academics* | • Literacy (128 supporting studies)<br>• Math (68 supporting studies)<br>• Science (17 supporting studies) |
| *Academic Vocabulary* | • Browder et al. (2009) research |
| *Daily Living* | • Person-centered planning<br>• Task analysis<br>• Self-management<br>• Social narratives |
| *Job and Community Skills* | • Technology<br>• Transition<br>• Job and community |
| *Self-Determination Skills* | • Decision making, choice making, self-management, self-advocacy, self-awareness, goal setting and problem solving |
| *Social and Communication* | • Social skills<br>• Communication skill needs |

## How to Teach

Browder et al. (2014) discussed evidence-based practices that emerged about how to teach students with severe disabilities. These are illustrated in Table 3.2, Additional Evidence-Based Strategies.

In addition, Table 3.3 gives an overview of considerations for teaching that is influenced by the great technical assistance work carried out by Florida Inclusion Network (FIN).

These considerations form the substance of the personalized pathways to learning upon which students with severe disabilities may travel. We will consider each of these considerations separately, but it is in their collective integration that intentional and thoughtful decisions about teaching and learning can be made.

### The Students' Scope and Pace of Learning Matches Their Learning Profile (Needs, Strengths and Preferences)

The first consideration relates to the amount and pace of content learning for students. Our students are able to learn standards-referenced curricula but we have to acknowledge that some of these learners learn a lot less content and follow a slower pace. This does not mean they cannot benefit from an enhanced content experience, but asks us to be flexible and responsive to the personalized needs of the student. We need to strike the challenging balance between individual learning needs, style and preferences and high expectations.

Table 3.2 Additional Evidence-Based Strategies

| Strategy | Information |
|---|---|
| Self-Directed Learning | Opportunities for self-directed learning so that students gain greater autonomy. |
| Pictorial Self-Instruction | Students with severe disabilities are taught to independently use picture activity schedules to complete tasks (Wong et al., 2015). |
| KWHL Charts | Guide students to identify: What they know (K); What they want to know (W); How to find out (H); What they learned (L) (Courtade et al., 2012). |
| Graphic Organizers | To identify question types and to independently answer *wh* questions (e.g., *where* asks for a place) about a text selection (Bethune & Wood, 2013). |
| Peer Tutors | A peer tutor—typically a same-age student from a general education classroom—delivers instruction to a student with disabilities—the tutee. |
| Technology | The use of technology to teach skills to students with severe disabilities has a moderate to strong evidence base depending on the type of technology. |
| Video Prompting | Video prompting shows clips of each component of a target behavior. |
| Video Modeling | A video is used to model the entire skill (Bellini, Peters, & Benner, 2007). |
| Computer-Assisted Instruction | Computer-assisted instruction (CAI) has been shown to have a moderate impact (Ayres, Mechling, & Sansosti, 2013). |

### The Student's Participation Reflects Information From His/Her Individual Educational Plan and Other Sources

All students with severe disabilities will have an IEP that sets out their personal learning goals. These are crucial in the creation of a personalized learning profile that reflects the needs, strengths and preferences of the student. These goals and objectives may well look like SMART targets (Specific, Measurable, Assessable, Realistic and Time limited) in order to be very focused and specific.

We may also develop curriculum-focused goals that apply to curriculum standards. There may be confluence between curriculum-focused and IEP

*Table 3.3* Teaching and Learning Considerations

| *Teaching and Learning Considerations* |
| --- |
| 1. The students' scope and pace of learning matches their learning profile (needs, strengths and preferences). |
| 2. The students' participation reflects information from their individual educational plan and other sources. |
| 3. Learning goals are meaningful for the students now and in the future. |
| 4. The need for explicit and systematic instruction of new skills. |
| 5. The need to provide more time to learn and practice skills. |
| 6. Students are learning priority skills in natural settings throughout the day and there are opportunities to apply skills in natural settings. Students have opportunities to interact and learn with typically developing peer and/or peers who are more able and participate in varied instructional groupings. |
| 7. Progress towards IEP goals/objectives and other curricular outcomes is measured and documented regularly. |
| 8. Age-appropriate instructional activities and materials enable active student participation. |
| 9. The need to provide reliable and flexible supports for learning, including the provision of modifications and accommodations as needed. |

focused targets, but there may not. In curriculum-focused engagement our approach to target setting may well differ. Lacey (2010) challenges the way we think about target setting for youngsters with severe disabilities as these learners are poor consumers of SMART targets. She suggests we should also think about targets that are SCRUFFY, which are:

- <u>S</u>tudent led
- <u>C</u>reative
- <u>R</u>elevant
- <u>U</u>nspecified
- <u>F</u>un
- <u>F</u>or
- <u>Y</u>oungsters

### *Learning Goals are Meaningful for the Student Now and in the Future*

District and school leaders, along with the multi-professional team, have the power to challenge historical practices to provide creative school systems that enable students to learn together in a Least Restrictive Environment (LRE). The LRE involves a move towards students with disabilities being "educated to the maximum extent appropriate with peers without disabilities" (Yell, 2006, p. 310); that is, inclusion in terms of placement and referred to as the Least Restrictive Environment. There has also been an emphasis on access to core academic general curriculum content (Turnbull, Wehmeyer & Shogren, 2010; Byers & Lawson, 2015); that is, inclusion in terms of curriculum. The second part of this book offers narratives of good practice that successfully reflect this.

We need to ensure that IEP goals are meaningful for the student now and in the future. It is important that the IEP team takes into account the "bigger picture" of the student's life and limit any dangerous assumptions about what IEP goals are to be developed for the student. This can be difficult when faced with a complex array of learning needs. Also, one must not forget to apply the concept of "Presumed Competence" discussed in Chapter 1.

*Systematic Instruction*

There is a need to develop explicit and systematic instructional opportunities for many students with severe disabilities. Literature reviews reflect a strong evidence base for using systematic instruction to teach academic skills (Browder et al., 2009; Parker & Schuster, 2002). We appreciate there is a legacy of effective systematic instruction for teaching daily living and community skills (Bambara, Koger, & Bartholomew, 2011). Recently, evidence has emerged that it is also effective for academic instruction (e.g., Browder et al., 2014). The components of systematic instruction are summarized in Table 3.4.

When designing instruction for teaching a skill, you first have to decide if the skill is discrete (can be performed by the student in one step), or chained (requires multiple steps to perform). Then, the data collection and response prompting techniques need to be decided. Browder et al. (2014) highlight that systematic instruction has a strong evidence base in supporting the teaching of community, daily living and academic skills to students with severe disabilities. Browder et al. (2014) contend that systematic instruction can be embedded in the general education classroom with careful planning and teamwork. Systematic instruction has three steps:

1   Define observable, measurable skill to be taught (can be obtained in one step or multiple steps).
2   Plan instruction and data collection.
3   Plan response prompting.

Systematic instruction can be blended with backward chaining to identify the different steps of a particular skill. Backward chaining is a process whereby early learning skills are broken down into small, distinct parts. Each step is taught in a very deliberate way, with prompting and reinforcement being applied as appropriate. Teachers can integrate varying ways to prompt and reinforce the learning.

Table 3.4 Systematic Instruction

| Component | Definition |
|---|---|
| Define the skill | Is it discrete or chained? |
| Collect data | The desired skill (whether discrete or chained) is entered on a data sheet for ongoing progress monitoring. |
| Prompting | Plan the response prompt and fading system to be used. |
| Simultaneous prompting | Where a prompt (e.g., verbal, model) is used alongside the targeted skill. This is eliminated after successful acquisition of skill. |
| Time delay | The prompt is used alongside the targeted skill and then faded with small steps over time. |
| Least intrusive prompts | The prompt is used only as needed to teach discrete or chained steps of the skill. |
| Most to least intrusive prompts | This is where the greatest prompt is given to begin with and gradually reduced. |
| Reinforcement | Instruction must also include reinforcement for correct responses. Reinforcement should always include praise and, depending on the motivational needs of the student, tangibles too. |
| Generalization | It is essential to teach for generalization. One way to promote generalization is to teach in contexts in which skills are most likely to occur naturally. Another way is to teach with multiple exemplars. |

## PROMPTING

Prompting follows a continuum of support ranging from a "most to least" level of prompting needed for the student to succeed. An example of a greatest level of prompting is called "hand-over-hand" where the teacher physically moves the student through the learning. An example of a minimum level of prompting is where the teacher simply waits with a reassuring proximity to the student and then offers a verbal prompt to the student to start the task. Prompting can be physical, gestural or verbal and is a very powerful support for learning. It is an evidence-based strategy identified by Browder et al. (2014) who found that, when teachers pay attention to prompting and are deliberate in their use of it, the students benefit.

REINFORCEMENT

Reinforcement is where an event or activity occurs after a learner engages in a desired behavior, which leads to the increased incidence of the behavior in the future. Reinforcement can come in the form of tangible rewards: time with a favorite toy, verbal praise from the teacher or a subtler acknowledgement between adult and student. Tangible reinforcement can occur immediately after the desired event or can be delayed, when the student builds up to the reward through the combining of a number of (usually similar) responses. For example, the student receives one smiley face for 4 minutes of on-task behavior, across the teaching session. The student collects smiley faces and at the end of the session receives an agreed reward, depending on the number of smiley faces. One smiley face may give access to 2 minutes of a desired video game, two smiley faces gives access to 6 minutes. Of course, we know rewards are much more influential when they are built on strong relationships between adults and student. We also appreciate that external rewards play a role in all our lives: we do non-preferred activities but follow with a preferred one, e.g., plan to finish the IEP reports and then plan a trip to the cinema. However, we do not spend all our lives in this way. We have intrinsic motivation to complete some activities: even though we may not want to, we walk the dog because we love the dog!

The structured procedures detailed are effective in teaching students a predictable process for learning. In my experience, they create a zone of comfort where students know what is expected of them and what they need to do to be successful. However, in practice, life may be much more unstructured and confusing. It is important to pay attention to resilience building of students in these more unstructured settings. Clearly, the aim is for independent application of new skills and concepts by students, which offers a natural pathway to discussion of the next consideration.

### The Need to Provide More Time to Learn and Practice Skills

Learners with severe disabilities may process information at a slower pace, which is not unusual for many students in the typically developing population. This means that teachers must become aware of individual processing time and adjust teaching and learning with respect to this. Imagine playing a game of tennis, where you are returning the ball across to a partner and achieving a good flow in your game. Your focus is very much on the ball and the play, and you are managing to hang on in there, return the ball and engage in a rally. It is a good feeling. Now imagine, instead of one tennis ball coming across the net, there are two, three, four or five, or as soon as you have returned one ball another flies past your ear. Not such a good feeling. You have just too much information to process. You would be fine if there were one ball in an expected pattern, but too many balls and you cannot pass one ball back. Or, think about being given a driving instruction in an unfamiliar town by your trusted GPS system in the car, "Turn left in 50 yards." You are taking in this information, preparing to turn left and the GPS follows up with another instruction, "Do a U turn." You immediately become confused...do you turn left or do a U turn? You have just too little time to process the information you have been given. Jean Ware (1996) carried out seminal communication research in classrooms of learners with profound disabilities. She videoed interactions between adults and learners, where the learners had significant issues in shared communication. She employed video analysis and not only looked at the video of the actual interaction but kept the video running on the students after the adult had moved along to another student. This research found that many students responded to the adult request for communicative interaction long after the adult had moved away. It is important for teachers of students with severe disabilities to become more aware of the personalized response rates of individual students.

### The Student is Learning Priority Skills in Natural Settings Throughout the Day and There Are Opportunities to Apply Skills in Natural Settings

It is indeed often a challenge to integrate individual goals across the different activities in an enriching and lively classroom. One strategy that can be employed to support the integration of individual student objectives and curriculum-focused enriched activities is an infused grid. An infused grid is a planning document that sets out where students' IEP targets are going to be met throughout the school day (Beech et al., 2002). Table 3.5, Format for Infused Grid, illustrates how an infused grid can be built to show where and when explicit instruction of new skills will occur, opportunities for the student to apply skills learned and when data will be collected about student performance. In the first column IEP goals are stated and in the second column each classroom/curricular opportunity on offer is stated.

The infused grid creates an instructional map for each student. It has already been established in this chapter that students with severe disabilities require explicit instruction of new skills. We cannot possibly explicitly teach all students every goal of their IEP in every curricular opportunity across the school day. In the infused grid, the educator marks with an "EI" that this is the curricular opportunity where there will be some explicit and very structured instruction around a specific IEP goal. Similar decisions will be made about opportunities where the student will apply their IEP skills in a more generalized way. The educator marks

Table 3.5 Format for Infused Grid

| Student: | | | Classroom Curricular Opportunities | | | |
|----------|----------|-----|-------|------|---------|------|
| IEP goals | Bellwork | ELA | Music | Math | Science | P.E. |
| 1. | | | | | | |
| 2. | | | | | | |
| 3. | | | | | | |
| 4. | | | | | | |

Key: EI = explicit instruction, G = apply skill generally, D = data collection.

these opportunities with a "G." The final part of the infused grid is where the educator decides where data will be collected around student performance, either in an explicit instruction or generalized engagement setting. Planned data collection is marked with a "D." It is important that data on how a student is responding to the IEP target and/or a curriculum target is collected. Each data collection point may look different because of this. There will be more discussion of this when formative and summative assessment is discussed. Table 3.6 is an example of a completed infused grid for a first grader, Charlene.

The classroom teacher teaches ELA, Math and Science. There are two "specials" teachers who teach Music and P.E. For Charlene, it was decided that explicit instruction for the first IEP target (matching 3D shapes) was to occur twice across the day: first with the initial Bellwork, as she arrives earlier than other students, and also during the Math session. Charlene will also have structured opportunities to practice matching 3D shapes in Music and P.E. Accordingly, Charlene's classroom teacher negotiated how she can have access to natural opportunities to practice this skill in the classes. The classroom teacher provided a set of simple 3D shapes for use in Music and P.E. Data related to how Charlene responded to this target are collected during Math and P.E. During P.E., the classroom assistant collected the data.

## Progress Towards IEP Goals/Objectives and Other Curricular Outcomes is Measured and Documented Regularly

Having worked hard to develop IEPs that include meaningful goals for the student it is essential that student performance and progress are documented. Completing the infused grid offers opportunities to collect selected data on how Charlene is progressing on specific IEP goals. It is important that data collection is focused and selective in order to generate manageable information about how the student is responding. Too much

Table 3.6 Infused Grid for Charlene

| Student: Charlene | Classroom Curricular Opportunities | | | | | |
|---|---|---|---|---|---|---|
| IEP goals | Bellwork | ELA | Music | Math | Science | P.E. |
| 1. Matches 3D shapes (circle, square, triangle). | EI | | G | EI D | | G D |
| 2. Responds to one part verbal request (with pictorial symbol prompt). | EI D | G | EI | | G D | G |
| 3. Holds book in correct way and turns pages. | G | EI D | G D | G | G | |
| 4. Matches six familiar words. | G | EI D | G | | G D | |

Key: EI = explicit instruction, G = apply skill generally, D = data collection.

data and the process becomes overwhelming. Too little data and the teacher does not have enough information to make an informed judgment. Teachers may choose to focus data collection on a specific IEP target across curricular experiences or focus on the specific IEP targets engaged within a curriculum experience. Student performance and progress data are collected for many reasons, both summative and formative. Data collected through the infused grid tool can meet both of these purposes if sustained over time.

### The Student has Opportunities to Interact and Learn with Typically Developing Peers and/or Peers Who are More Able and Participates in Varied Instructional Groupings

This consideration is concerned with the learning groupings teachers may plan for a student with severe disabilities. Historically, this group of learners has highly personalized learning pathways that tend to be very individualized. We know that the experience of learning in a group creates an environment for social learning that may positively contribute to the learning of all members, even if the members bring varied skill sets, learning needs and preferences (Whiten & Erdal, 2012). Many students with severe disabilities will present as highly individualized learners, and there will be times when learning in a very individualized way is highly appropriate. This particular consideration asks us to enrich individualized learning with opportunities to work in a variety of groups with a variety of other learners. In a project that gathered the perspectives of young children, some of whom had labels of autism, Jones and Gillies (2010) found that children have strong preferences to work alone or in a group. However, what was important to them was that they had a choice as to whether to work alone or in a group. The children stated clearly that they did not like to be made to work alone by an adult.

### Age-Appropriate Instructional Activities and Materials Enable Active Student Participation

It is important to remember that, as a student progresses through school, the instructional activities and materials also evolve. Gone are the days that we present teenagers with baby toys because we are trying to match their conceptual level to materials. We may have a teenager who is in need of fundamental skill building in early Mathematics. Our challenge is to meet these fundamental needs in enhanced curricular experiences. (The shared narratives in the second section of this book demonstrate how this can be done.) It is also important to enable students to be actively engaged in their own learning, not passive recipients. This can be a challenge to facilitate when students show a range of response levels from dampened to hyperactive. The more we get to know our students and learn about their particular participation levels, the more success we will have in facilitating more active participation. Assistive technology and the advances that have been made in this area have offered teachers choices in mediating student learning in a motivating way. For example, research is demonstrating the value of integrating iPads into instruction for students with disabilities (Desai et al., 2014).

### The Need to Provide Reliable and Flexible Supports for Learning, Including the Provision of Modifications and Accommodations as Needed

This consideration is concerned with the way the curriculum is planned and presented for students with severe disabilities. Any modifications and accommodations must be included in the IEP and must also be represented in all learning and assessment activities. Modifications refer to the changes that are made to the curriculum. For example, a modified curriculum may follow similar areas of numeracy and literacy to the general education curriculum, but at a greatly different level and/or pace. A modified curriculum could also be partial completion of general education requirements or alternative goals, which may be based on functional life skills or vocational curricula goals. Sometimes relatively simple accommodations can enable students with severe disabilities to participate in classroom activities and learn the same skills as their typical peers. At other times, students with significant disabilities may need more substantial accommodations to enable them to participate actively in instructional activities. Accommodations can be provided in different ways that relate to the areas of methods and materials, assignments and assessments, learning environment, time demands, scheduling and any communication system the student may use (Beech et al., 2002). Accommodations provided in any of these areas should be based on the needs of the student and an analysis of learning requirements and environmental demands, in order to promote active participation and the highest degree of independence possible. Accommodations relating to methods and materials for instruction may include the use of prompting, visuals and objects of reference, and refer to considerations of how learning materials are adapted or augmented with technology to promote the active engagement of the student. Prompting is hierarchical, moving from most to least use of prompting. When a skill is being introduced the educator may rely heavily on a great deal of prompting to establish success. However, the use of support prompts should be regularly monitored with the intention of lessening the prompts to encourage independent, successful responses from the student. Accommodations relating to assignments and assessments involve the way students are supported to express or communicate their learning. In relation to accommodations, a student who is unable to write may answer questions orally read aloud by a paraprofessional. Students may also express their thoughts using stamps, pictures or specialized picture/ word processing software. Accommodations relating to the learning environment may include adaptations for physical accessibility, specialized equipment, instructional grouping, classroom management and behavioral support. This may involve making thoughtful decisions about positioning of the student around the physical space of the classroom. Instructional grouping may include one-to-one instruction, peer-mediated learning or the need for small group learning. As mentioned in a previous section, instructional grouping is more effective when it is fluid and tailored to individual student needs, strengths and preferences. All modifications and accommodations should be enrichment focused rather than remediation focused.

Although these considerations relate to students with severe disabilities, it is accepted that all students in schools display particular preferences in learning that are represented in multiple intelligence research and practice. Howard Gardner's seminal work on multiple intelligences proposed seven intelligences that can be multiple and co-exist (Smith, 2002, 2008). In pedagogical decision-making these multiple intelligences may also be important to consider. The eight intelligences are:

- Linguistic
- Logical-mathematical
- Musical
- Bodily-kinesthetic
- Spatial
- Interpersonal
- Intrapersonal
- Naturalistic

Please note that an eighth intelligence, "naturalistic", was recently added to the original list of seven (OASIS, 2017). It is important to remember that learners with severe disabilities may also have preferences that are represented across the multiple intelligences and that this can impact the way that learning is presented and mediated by the teacher.

## Conclusion

This chapter began by setting out the crucial role of multi-professional working when teaching students with severe disabilities. Key considerations of teaching and learning for this group of students were then discussed. These considerations may inform the decisions made about teaching and learning for students with severe disabilities. They are considerations over which every teacher of every student deliberates. However, the strategies inherent in the consideration may be much more explicit and have a more intense application for students with severe disabilities. These considerations indeed play an important symbiotic relationship with each other.

# Chapter 4

# What Are Curriculum Content Standards?

Standards are "general statements of what students should know or be able to do as a result of their public school education" (McGregor, 2003, p. 34). Curriculum content standards represent the expectations of the general education curriculum. They can be further broken down and described as benchmarks and performance standards (McGregor, 2003). Curriculum content standards encompass what gets taught, including skills, knowledge and subject matter. Benchmarks are "clear descriptions of expectations for student knowledge, skills and abilities relative to content standards" (McGregor, 2003, p. 34). Performance standards illustrate a student's current level of skill, knowledge or ability relative to benchmarks.

Curriculum content standards set targets and performance levels that students should achieve in the content (Nolet & McLaughlin, 2005). NCLB (2002) was the first mandate that all states need to have one set of curriculum content standards and achievement standards (Towles-Reeves & Kleniert, 2006). According to Nolet and McLaughlin (2005), standards are important for several reasons: they create equity across schools by defining what teachers should teach, define what content should be taught and assessed, and align state curriculum standards directly to curricular frameworks, materials and goals.

In the standards themselves, there is integrated Content Complexity. Content complexity reflects features such as prior knowledge, processing of concepts and skills, sophistication, number of parts and application of content structure required to meet a particular content standard. The content complexity built into this state's standards are:

- Low—recall.
- Moderate—basic application of skills and concepts.
- High—strategic thinking and complex reasoning.

There is a distinction between *standards-referenced* and *standards-based* curriculum. *Standards-referenced* curriculum means that what gets taught or tested is "referenced" to or derived from learning standards (i.e., standards are the source of the content and skills taught to students—the original "reference" for the lesson). In a standards-referenced system, teaching and testing are guided by standards; in a standards-based system, teachers work to ensure that students actually learn the expected material as they progress in their education.

It is not unusual for students with significant cognitive disabilities to access the general education curriculum through alternative achievement standards (Towles-Reeves & Kleniert, 2006). Alternative achievement standards "define student performance that differs from a grade-level achievement standards in terms of complexity, but these achievement standards must be aligned with a state's regular academic content standards, promote access to the general education curriculum, and reflect high or challenging standards" (Nolet & McLaughlin, 2005, p. 5).

## Developing the Context for the Teachers' Narratives

Access points of state content standards form the point of reference for the teachers in this book. Each state may differ in its name or approach to accessing the state standards for learners with severe disabilities. Therefore, the curriculum standards discussed in this chapter may not represent all states, only the state in which the teachers, who have contributed to the book, work. However, in any state you will find a standards-referenced curriculum for students with the most significant cognitive disabilities who are deemed eligible under IDEA (2004). In this particular state, access points make up this curriculum, which has been developed for students who follow a modified curriculum as agreed by the IEP team. There are access points for all subjects of the standards curriculum: these subjects are English Language Arts (ELA), Mathematics, Science, Social Studies, Dance, Health Education, Physical Education, Music, Theatre, Visual Art and Health Education. The teachers teach lessons that may cover multiple subjects. However, their narratives focus on ELA or Mathematics to highlight how they are engaging in these subjects in an enhanced and purposeful way.

Access points are extensions of the general content standards with reduced levels of complexity. The aim is to connect students with significant cognitive disabilities to state-referenced content standards. The goal of the access points remains focused on college, career and community readiness for all students.

In this particular state, the content standards for ELA and Mathematics are organized in slightly different ways. This influences the way access points are also organized. ELA knowledge is represented structurally in a strand, cluster, standard and access point hierarchy. For ELA, a strand refers to a particular body of knowledge in the subject. In ELA the strands are: Reading, Writing, Speaking & Listening and Language. In each strand there are clusters of related content standards (www.fldoe.org/core/fileparse.php/7539/urlt/lafsqrg.pdf). Table 4.1 details the strands and clusters for ELA at each grade level.

For Mathematics, the scenario is a little more complex; the term domain is used instead of strand. Domains represent key components that make up the main components of the content standards. Across K–12 Mathematics there are some domains that relate to the whole age range and some domains that relate to specific age ranges (as illustrated in Table 4.2). Each domain has a number of clusters, which are groups of related standards. In further review, multiple clusters are organized into Major, Supporting and Additional to represent their importance to the domain, which gives an indication of emphasis of teaching rather than the exclusion of specific clusters. The navigation of the Mathematics standards is a challenging process. Table 4.2 details the domains for Mathematics at each grade level.

Information on grade level clusters for each domain can be located at: www.cpalms.org/Uploads/docs/FrontMatter/mafs_structure_coding_explanation.pdf

Each strand/domain and cluster then details content standards, which all students follow and upon which they are assessed. For example, Table 4.3 illustrates the content standards for Kindergarten Language Arts; Strand: Reading Standards for Literature; Cluster 1: Key Ideas and Details.

Likewise, Table 4.4 details the content standards for 5th Grade Mathematics, Domain Geometry, Cluster 1.

Each standard is broken down into graduated steps in the form of access points. The number of access points for each standard varies. For example, Table 4.5 shows the access points for Kindergarten Language Arts; Strand: Reading Standards for Literature; Cluster 1: Standard 2, "With prompting and support, retell familiar stories, including key details."

The access points for Mathematics are structured in a similar hierarchical way. Table 4.6 shows the access points for 5th Grade Mathematics, Domain Geometry, Cluster 1, Standard 1.

As illustrated across the tables, the access points represent multiple steps for each content strand/domain, cluster and standard. This creates a very large state standards document and cumulatively presents an enormous challenge for teachers to navigate simply and process the access points. However, there are resources that have been developed across states that are intended to help teachers in this endeavor. For example, the multi-state collaborative around common core connectors.

Table 4.1 Strands and Clusters for ELA at Each Grade Level

| Grade Level | Strands | Clusters |
|---|---|---|
| Kindergarten | Reading for Informational Text<br>Reading for Literature<br>Foundational Skills<br>Writing<br>Speaking and Listening<br>Language | Key Ideas and Details<br>Craft and Structure<br>Integration of Knowledge and Ideas<br>Range of Reading and Level of Text<br>  Complexity<br>Print Concepts<br>Phonological Awareness<br>Phonics and Word Recognition<br>Fluency<br>Text Types and Purposes<br>Production and Distribution of<br>  Writing<br>Research to Build and Present<br>  Knowledge<br>Comprehension and Collaboration<br>Presentation of Knowledge and Ideas<br>Conventions of Standard English<br>Vocabulary Acquisition and Use |
| 1st Grade | Reading for Informational Text<br>Reading for Literature<br>Foundational Skills<br>Writing<br>Speaking and Listening<br>Language | Key Ideas and Details<br>Craft and Structure<br>Integration of Knowledge and Ideas<br>Range of Reading and Level of Text<br>  Complexity<br>Print Concepts<br>Phonological Awareness<br>Phonics and Word Recognition<br>Fluency<br>Text Types and Purposes<br>Production and Distribution of<br>  Writing<br>Research to Build and Present<br>  Knowledge<br>Comprehension and Collaboration<br>Presentation of Knowledge and Ideas<br>Conventions of Standard English<br>Vocabulary Acquisition and Use |
| 2nd Grade | Reading for Informational Text<br>Reading for Literature<br>Foundational Skills<br>Writing<br>Speaking and Listening<br>Language | Key Ideas and Details<br>Craft and Structure<br>Integration of Knowledge and Ideas<br>Range of Reading and Level of Text<br>  Complexity<br>Phonics and Word Recognition<br>Fluency<br>Text Types and Purposes<br>Production and Distribution of<br>  Writing<br>Research to Build and Present<br>  Knowledge |

*Table 4.1* Continued

| Grade Level | Strands | Clusters |
|---|---|---|
| | | Comprehension and Collaboration |
| | | Presentation of Knowledge and Ideas |
| | | Conventions of Standard English |
| | | Knowledge of Language |
| | | Vocabulary Acquisition and Use |
| 3rd Grade<br>4th Grade<br>5th Grade | Reading for Informational Text<br>Reading for Literature<br>Foundational Skills<br>Writing<br>Speaking and Listening<br>Language | Reading (for Informational Text *and* for Literature)<br>Key Ideas and Details<br>Craft and Structure<br>Integration of Knowledge and Ideas<br>Range of Reading and Level of Text Complexity<br>Foundational Skills<br>Phonics and Word Recognition<br>Fluency<br>Writing<br>Text Types and Purposes<br>Production and Distribution of Writing<br>Research to Build and Present Knowledge<br>Range of Writing<br>Speaking & Listening<br>Comprehension and Collaboration<br>Presentation of Knowledge and Ideas<br>Language<br>Conventions of Standard English<br>Knowledge of Language<br>Vocabulary Acquisition and Use |
| 6th Grade<br>7th Grade<br>8th Grade<br>9th Grade<br>10th Grade<br>11th Grade<br>12th Grade | Reading for Informational Text<br>Reading for Literature<br>Writing<br>Speaking and Listening<br>Language | Key Ideas and Details<br>Craft and Structure<br>Integration of Knowledge and Ideas<br>Range of Reading and Level of Text Complexity<br>Text Types and Purposes<br>Production and Distribution of Writing<br>Research to Build and Present Knowledge<br>Range of Writing<br>Comprehension and Collaboration<br>Presentation of Knowledge and Ideas<br>Conventions of Standard English<br>Knowledge of Language<br>Vocabulary Acquisition and Use |

*Table 4.2* Domains for Mathematics at Each Grade Level

| Grade | Domain |
|---|---|
| Kindergarten | Counting and Cardinality<br>Geometry<br>Measurement and Data<br>Number and Operations in Base Ten<br>Operations and Algebraic Thinking |
| 1st, 2nd, 3rd, 4th<br>and 5th Grade | Geometry<br>Measurement and Data<br>Number and Operations in Base Ten<br>Operations and Algebraic Thinking |
| 6th and 7th Grade | Expressions & Equations<br>Geometry<br>Ratios & Proportional Relationships<br>Statistics & Probability<br>The Number System |
| 8th Grade | Expressions & Equations<br>Functions<br>Geometry<br>Statistics & Probability<br>The Number System |
| 9th, 10th, 11th<br>and 12th Grade | Algebra: Arithmetic with Polynomials & Rational Expressions<br>Algebra: Creating Equations<br>Algebra: Reasoning with Equations & Inequalities<br>Algebra: Seeing Structure in Expressions<br>Calculus<br>Functions: Building Functions<br>Functions: Interpreting Functions<br>Functions: Linear, Quadratic & Exponential Models<br>Functions: Trigonometric Functions<br>Geometry: Circles<br>Geometry: Congruence<br>Geometry: Expressing Geometric Properties with Equations<br>Geometry: Geometric Measurement & Dimension<br>Geometry: Modeling with Geometry<br>Geometry: Similarity, Right Triangles & Trigonometry<br>Number & Quantity: Quantities<br>Number & Quantity: The Complex Number System<br>Number & Quantity: The Real Number System<br>Number & Quantity: Vector & Matrix Quantities<br>Statistics & Probability: Conditional Probability & the Rules of Probability<br>Statistics & Probability: Interpreting Categorical & Quantitative Data<br>Statistics & Probability: Making Inferences & Justifying Conclusions<br>Statistics & Probability: Using Probability to Make Decisions |

*Table 4.3* Content Standards Kindergarten Language Arts; Strand: Reading Standards for Literature; Cluster 1: Key Ideas and Details

---

*Kindergarten ELA*
*Cluster 1: Key Ideas and Details*

*Standard 1.* With prompting and support, ask and answer questions about key details in a text.

*Standard 2.* With prompting and support, retell familiar stories, including key details.

*Standard 3.* With prompting and support, identify characters, settings and major events in a story.

---

*Table 4.4* Content Standards for Mathematics, Domain Geometry, Cluster 1—5th Grade

---

*5th Grade Mathematics*
*Domain Geometry*

*Cluster 1: Graph points on the coordinate plane to solve real-world and mathematical problems.*

1. Use a pair of perpendicular number lines, called axes, to define a coordinate system, with the intersection of the lines (the origin) arranged to coincide with the 0 on each line and a given point in the plane located by using an ordered pair of numbers, called its coordinates. Understand that the first number indicates how far to travel from the origin in the direction of one axis, and the second number indicates how far to travel in the direction of the second axis, with the convention that the names of the two axes and the coordinates correspond (e.g., x-axis and x-coordinate, y-axis and y-coordinate).

2. Classify two-dimensional figures into categories based on their properties.

---

*Table 4.5* Kindergarten Language Arts; Strand: Reading Standards for Literature; Cluster 1: Key Ideas and Details. Standards. Access Points.

---

*Strand: Reading Standards for Literature*

*Standard 2.* With prompting and support, retell familiar stories, including key details.

*Access Points*

| | |
|---|---|
| LAFS.K.RL.1.AP.2a | With prompting and support, retell a favorite story, including key details. |
| LAFS.K.RL.1.AP.2b | With prompting and support, sequence a set of events in a familiar story. |
| LAFS.K.RL.1.AP.2c | With prompting and support, identify the beginning, middle and ending of a familiar story. |
| LAFS.K.RL.1.AP.2d | Retell a familiar story (e.g., What was the story about?). |

*Table 4.6* Access Points for 5th Grade Mathematics, Domain Geometry, Cluster 1, Standard 1

---

*Domain: Geometry*

*Cluster:* Graph points on the coordinate plane to solve real-world and mathematical problems.

*Standard 1.* Use a pair of perpendicular number lines, called axes, to define a coordinate system, with the intersection of the lines (the origin) arranged to coincide with the 0 on each line and a given point in the plane located by using an ordered pair of numbers, called its coordinates. Understand that the first number indicates how far to travel from the origin in the direction of one axis, and the second number indicates how far to travel in the direction of the second axis, with the convention that the names of the two axes and the coordinates correspond (e.g., x-axis and x-coordinate, y-axis and y-coordinate).

*Access Points*

| | |
|---|---|
| MAFS.5.G.1.AP.1a | Locate the x- and y- axis on a coordinate plane. |
| MAFS.5.G.1.AP.1b | Locate points on a coordinate plane. |
| MAFS.5.G.1.AP.1c | Graph ordered pairs (coordinates). |

## Common Core Connectors

The National Center and State Collaborative (NCSC) is a project led by five centers and twenty-four states, building an alternative assessment based on alternative achievement standards for students with the most significant cognitive disabilities (NCSC, 2015). The intent of the project is to support students with the most significant cognitive disabilities to achieve increasingly higher academic outcomes and leave high school ready for post-secondary options. The resources developed for schools and teachers are aligned to the Common Core State Standards (CCSS). The resources include materials in two broad areas:

- Curriculum Resources developed to enhance understanding of curriculum content.
- Instructional Resources related specifically to classroom teaching.

In these two broad areas we see professional development materials aimed at parents and teachers that support and explain the teaching and assessment of the standards. Included in Curriculum Resources is a Communication Tool Kit, which is a series of professional development modules aimed at high-quality communication intervention. Two Instructional Resources deserve a mention here. They are, Instructional Families and Element Cards. Instructional Families are visual representations of curricular emphasis within and across grade bands. These are presented as a graphic and assist awareness of the standards and the relationship across standards. Instructional Families are presented in three different ways:

- By grade band and curricular domain and cluster.
- By each grade and curricular standard.
- By Instructional Family and curricular standard.

Element Cards present multiple perspectives of instruction of the targeted curricular content. Each Element Card contains one or more curricular standards, strands, domains, clusters and progress indicators. Element Cards are aligned to the state curricular standards and incorporate principles of Universal Design for Learning (UDL), an approach to curriculum development that makes instruction and assessment accessible for all learners. UDL principles offer recommendations for building a curriculum that utilizes multiple means of presentation and allows the learner to work and respond in a format that meets their needs for learning and expression.

Access points and associated resources are intended to represent different levels of graduated engagement and understanding:

- At a concrete level where the experience is very concrete or hands-on and represents learning that begins a student's interactions with the grade level curriculum.
- At a representational level where the learner associates meaning with symbols and print.
- At an abstract level.

The teachers in the classrooms of Chapters 5 through to 10 make explicit reference to the access points when they plan lessons. However, there are other curricular influences that influence their decision-making, particularly in relation to personalized student IEP targets.

## Other Curriculum Influences

Teachers talked about a range of curricular influences in relation to personalized target setting that go beyond the access points. For this group of teachers it tended to be in the areas of communication, technology, early intellectual development, movement and vocational skills. The influences that the teachers shared include:

- Their own individual knowledge and experience about what the student "needs" to be successful. This was described as something intuitive and based on their experience with students with disabilities. Five out of the six teachers shared that this knowledge base was influenced by their teacher preparation experiences.

- Collaboration with the speech and language therapist on all communication goals. All the teachers discussed working in close partnership with the speech and language therapists and relied on the professional expertise of their colleagues in relation to communication and Alternative Augmentative Communication (AAC).
- AAC devices that have their own hierarchical programs and the ability for teachers and speech therapists to personalize the programs for individual students.
- Collaboration with the occupational therapist on all switch-related goals, particularly in relation to type of positioning of the switch.
- Collaboration with the physical therapist on all movement goals.
- Collaboration with healthcare professionals on the medical needs of the students. This mostly related to medical issues related to positioning and eating.
- Collaboration with specialist district teachers. For example, the teacher for students with visual impairment suggested the use of a program for Joy, whom we will meet in Chapter 9. The Complexity Sequence Kit (CVI) is a resource, published by the American Printing House for the Blind. The IEP goal for Joy was written directly from the goals provided by the kit. The sequence of cards used is designed to build upon skills and present more and more visually complex illustrations as the student improves in her skills. This is helping Joy to identify and locate familiar images, even when they are presented with an increasing number of distracting background elements.
- i-Ready Diagnostics, which is a published grade level instruction and practice program for English Language Arts, Writing and Mathematics that prepares students for the state standards. The program provides teachers with a step-by-step, point-of-use guide to teach the standards.
- Unique Learning System® is an online, standards-based set of interactive tools designed for students with special needs to access the general curriculum. Unique Learning System provides preschool through transition students with standards-based materials specifically designed to meet their instructional needs.
- Reading Wonders is a reading program designed specifically for the Common Core State Standards for Reading/Language Arts.
- In-school program designed around a work lab center. This includes a hierarchy of functional and vocational skills.

## Conclusion

This chapter has given an introduction to the curriculum standards specific to the state in which the teachers represented in Chapters 5 to 10 teach. Information about access points is also presented, with examples from ELA Kindergarten and 5th Grade Mathematics. An example of the resources available to teachers in this state is shared. The chapter has also discussed other curricular influences that this group of teachers shared that inform their decision-making. This sets the curricular context of the narratives of lessons the teachers chose to share to represent one of their best curricular referenced lessons.

# Section II

## Introduction

This section of the book contains narratives of favorite lessons by six teachers who work with students with severe/significant disabilities. All teachers teach learners in more restricted settings but ensure that their students engage in standards-referenced enhanced learning. The research for this section took over a year of working collaboratively with each teacher to share their stories in structured and accessible ways. To honor the commitment and contribution of the teachers, the chapters in this section are written with the teachers and not for them. Therefore they share the authorship of the chapters. The chapters represent ELA and Math lessons at the elementary, middle and high school level.

The teachers work in two different schools in a South Eastern American State. Information about each school is included here to avoid repetition. All student and school names are anonymous, but we have the support of families to include their children in these stories and photographs to be shared.

In each chapter, there is a section where the reasons the teacher believes this was an effective lesson are shared. These are presented in the first person to connect with the reader more powerfully.

## Introduction to the Schools

### Orchard Hill School Written With Robin Myers

Orchard Hill School serves 190 students with significant intellectual disabilities. They range in age from 3 to 22 years and are in grades pre-K through 12th Grade. Orchard Hill was purpose-built in 2008 to accommodate the educational needs of the county's Exceptional Student Education population. In addition to being individuals with significant intellectual disabilities, many of the students may have co-existing issues. The staff of Orchard Hill consists of 30 teachers, 52 paraprofessionals,

2 administrators (1 principal and 1 assistant principal) and 7 professional licensed staff (1 Board Certified Behavior Analyst (BCBA), 1 behavior resource teacher, 2 registered nurses, 2 occupational therapists and 1 physical therapist).

In 2008, Orchard Hill School developed a plan to transition from primarily teaching functional skills to teaching academics. Elements of the plan included the development of an intensive school-based training program for the school's teachers and teacher assistants. This evolution was a proactive response to the changing landscape of curriculum entitlement for students with significant cognitive disabilities, which increasingly embraced standards-referenced curricula. In addition to a focus upon instructional strategies, Orchard Hill also addressed curricular elements in line with the state's curricular access point directives. Scope and Sequence documents were developed for every access point course in grades K through 12th. In addition, the school developed a unit-by-unit instructional framework that included many of the Marzano strategies of effective instruction for all students (Marzano, 2001). Evaluation and progress monitoring was aligned by topic for all grade levels. Orchard Hill School has been recognized as leading the charge in terms of successfully teaching state access points to students with severe and significant disabilities. Ongoing mentoring and coaching visits from personnel from districts and schools across the state attest to this. Chapters 5, 7, 8 and 9 are based in Orchard Hill School.

### Spring Park School Written With Edwina Oliver

Spring Park School is an Exceptional Student Education (ESE) center school, which serves students from Pre-K to age 22 in a suburban mid-sized school district. It is a purpose-built one-story building with a wide range of services and therapies, including physical therapy, occupational therapy, speech and language therapy, vision therapy, hearing services, assistive and augmentative communication services, social work services, counseling services, adaptive physical education, music, art, horticulture, hippotherapy (horses), aquatic therapy, scouts, vocational training both on and off campus, job coaching, OJT (On the Job Training), community based instruction, social skills training programs, behavior modification programs and nursing services.

The school has five academic teams that have discrete responsibility for teaching groups of learners. The school is physically organized around the teams so that a corridor of classrooms, or part of the school building, houses the teams. The teams are:

- The A.C.T.I.O.N. Team
- The TRANSITION Team K–8

- The TRANSITION Team 9–12+
- The SPECTRUM Team
- The DAT Team.

The A.C.T.I.O.N. Team (Acceptance, Courage, Tolerance, Individuality, Opportunity and Nurture) is made up of students in grades K through 8th with emotional behavioral disabilities receiving the standard academic curriculum. A social skills curriculum is embedded throughout their day. The goal is to modify behaviors in order that students attain the skills necessary to return to their district school. The TRANSITION Team K–8 works with students at points of transition in the school who are working on Access Point standards. The TRANSITION Team 9–12+ is made up of students who are working on Access Point standards and functional life skills. Both teams have multiple exceptionalities within these two teams. The SPECTRUM Team is made up primarily of students with Autism Spectrum Disorder with intellectual disabilities in grades K through 12th, with a few postgraduate students (Grade 12+) as well. All classrooms are highly structured with visual supports to address and monitor progress on communication and behavior needs. Finally, the DAT Team (Developmental Assistive Technology) is made up of students with severe and profound intellectual disabilities in grades K through 12th, which also includes postgraduate students. Between eight and ten of these students receive nursing services for feeding and require augmentative and assistive technology for communication in order to access the curriculum. Each of these academic teams have one to three paraprofessionals assigned to support students in the classrooms. Chapters 6 and 10 are based in Spring Park School. Chapter 6 is with a teacher in the DAT team and Chapter 10 is with a teacher from the TRANSITION Team 9–12+.

# Chapter 5

# Fact or Fiction

*With Vilmary Tautiva*

This lesson takes place at Orchard Hill School.

## The Classroom

There are eight students in the class, one teacher and two paraprofessionals. All students are on state Standard Access Points and have Individualized Education Plans (IEPs). The students are highly interactive even with limited mobility skills. The grade levels are 4th, 5th, 6th, 7th and 8th. Two students are non-verbal, three are verbal and three students have low speech intelligibility. The students are taught in 1:3 teacher to student ratio with low and high technology. The classroom follows an Orchard Hill Scope and Sequence that is aligned to the state standards. The materials selected for the academic lessons are standards-based.

## The Adults

Mrs. T., the class teacher, is a second career teacher. She has a Bachelor of Arts in Sociology, a Master of Arts in Special Education and an Educational Specialist in Leadership. She started as a paraprofessional in 2001 providing support for English Speaking Other Language (ESOL) students. In 2008, she became a teacher of pre-K students with disabilities. Following teaching pre-K, she taught a self-contained class of students with autism. The following summer she went to a special day school to teach Extended School Year (ESY) to students with severe disabilities and has since been teaching at the center school. Mrs. T. is on the school curriculum team, leadership team, School Advisory Committee (SAC) Safe Schools and is a new teacher mentor. Ms. J., one of the paraprofessionals, has a Bachelor of Science in Social Work. She has been a teacher assistant for the last 4 years. She has prior experience with high school students with disabilities. Mrs. S., the second paraprofessional, has a Bachelor of Arts in Psychology and is pursuing a Master of Arts in clinical psychology.

## The Students

Krystal is 10 years old and is identified under the disability categories of Intellectual Disability (InD) and Speech or Language Impairment (SLI). Krystal is mobile. She has a Behavior Intervention Plan (BIP) that targets minimizing physical and property aggression. Krystal has made significant progress in reducing meltdowns and increasing time on tasks. She is working on identifying the letters of her name, and increasing communication skills both academically and socially. Her priority educational need is to increase communication skills.

Her IEP goals are:

- Language and Literacy: to respond to "Wh" questions, "Who," "What," "Where" and "When" accurately.
- Math: to identify numbers 1–10.
- Personal Social Education: to take turns and increase tolerance time for non-preferred teacher-directed tasks.

Calvin is 10 years old and is identified under the disability categories of Intellectual Disability (InD) and Other Health Impairment (OHI). Calvin is mobile and verbal. He speaks in a very high volume for his small size. Calvin is very social. He loves to move constantly. Calvin learns best when he is allowed to have frequent movement breaks. His priority educational needs are to improve functional reading and Math skills. His current IEP needs are:

- Language and Literacy: Reading Comprehension—to answer "Wh" questions and use the text for reference.
- Math: to complete one-to-one correspondence.
- Personal Social Education: to increase independent time on task (4 minutes).

Kaley is 11 years old and she is identified under the disability category of Intellectual Disability (InD). She is on a Behavior Plan that in the past few months has demonstrated substantially reduced self-injurious and aggressive behaviors. She is mobile and verbal. Kaley learns best with clear, immediate consequences and when she is spoken to in a very low volume voice. Her priority educational needs are to express her emotions peacefully. Her IEP goals are:

- Language and Literacy: to respond to "Why" questions in reading comprehension.
- Math: to find combinations of 15 and identify missing numbers 80 percent of the time, with one visual or verbal prompt.
- Personal Social Education: to express her emotions peacefully.

Joaquin is 11 years old and is identified under the disability categories of Orthopedic Impairment (OI) and Speech or Language Impairment (SLI). Joaquin uses an electric chair. He likes to drive his chair very fast but has low motor function. He is an emerging communicator and uses an iPad with the TouchChat app to communicate. Joaquin also uses gestures to communicate. He is very witty. He requires adult support when eating and toileting. His priority educational needs are to communicate effectively through his device and make safe travel choices throughout the school campus.

His IEP goals are:

- To demonstrate safe navigation through the school campus using various wheeled mobility and using a safe speed.
- To use a preferred mode of communication to identify and describe key details independently.
- To raise his right hand to get teachers' attention independently.

Jarrett is 11 years old and is identified under the disability category of Autism Spectrum Disorder (ASD). Jarrett has developed verbal communication over the last few years. He is mobile. Jarrett loves science, music and technology. This year he has made progress in completing simple tasks when an adult explains the directions. His priority educational needs are to increase his coping skills for undesired tasks, increase his basic Math skills and develop personal hygiene routines.

His IEP goals are:

- To use text to respond to questions and add more details in his responses.
- To solve simple Math problems involving joining or separating sets of objects to 10, including basic coins (pennies, nickels and dimes), with visual and verbal cues 65 percent of the time.
- To attempt and complete work with fewer verbal outbursts of "Too much" and to ask for assistance in a calmer tone with no more than one verbal cue.

Robert is 11 years old and qualifies for services under Intellectual Disability (InD) and Speech or Language Impairment (SLI). He uses a wheelchair and requires adult support to meet all of his personal needs. His priority goal is to increase his social and academic responses verbally with less adult prompting.

His IEP goals are:

- To ask questions of peers using strategies to maximize speech intelligibility, such as sound approximations, slow rate and eye contact.

- To determine the correct value of coins (penny, nickel, dime and quarters) verbally and with the use of academic software with different coin combinations.
- To increase his self-advocacy skills.

Rafael is 14 years old, and qualifies for Other Health Impairment (OHI) and Speech or Language Impairment (SLI). He has a pacemaker and walks with the use of a walker. He is an emerging communicator and uses an iPad with the TouchChat app for communication. His hands tremble significantly and he takes additional time to respond. He requires adult support at mealtimes but makes a couple of attempts to feed himself and is able to toilet independently with minor assistance with fasteners. Rafael loves music. His priority educational needs are to develop increased independence in completing tasks and assignments, to understand a schedule and follow routines in the classroom.

His IEP goals are:

- To spontaneously use his communication device to request objects and/or activities, and to greet adults/peers.
- To identify all the letters of his first name and input them into his communication device.
- To demonstrate the value of 1–10.

Niabi is 15 years old and is identified under the disability category of Intellectual Disability (InD). There is also a question of ASD, but Mom has not provided the doctor's diagnosis. Niabi learns through pictures. She is verbal but difficult to understand. Her Spanish language is more advanced than her English, but she often gets Spanish and English mixed up. She is very social and likes to ask about family members' names and gets very concerned regarding peers' school attendance. Niabi responds better to academics with visuals than verbal responses. She is mobile and can independently meet her personal needs. Her priority educational need is to concentrate on the task she is working on for 10 minutes.

Her IEP goals are:

- To use six picture symbols representing language concepts (hot, cold, dirty, clean, on, off), to describe photographs independently, to match two words that are the same using visual or verbal cues, and to use a keyboard to type a given word correctly.
- To identify pennies, nickels, dimes and quarters.
- To increase task time and reduce frequency of getting up from seat to search for sensory input.

## Overview of Lesson

The lesson is an ELA lesson focused on teaching students the text structure of fiction and nonfiction stories. The students were provided with visuals of text features of fiction and nonfiction books. The books for the lesson were changed at the last minute when the class received the book *Elmer* by David McKee from Shriner's Burn Hospital in Cincinnati, Ohio. One of the students in the class had spent 2 months there recovering from an injury. The book was incorporated into the lesson with a nonfiction elephant book to provide emotional support to this student who had been burned.

## Lesson Learning Goal

Students will explore the differences between fiction and nonfiction. They will compare and contrast different genres and their literary devices.

## Lesson Objectives

### Essential Understanding: (Concrete)

- To identify a literary device.
- To build grade-appropriate vocabulary using strategies including context clues and study of word parts.

### Essential Understanding: (Representation)

- To analyze how authors use literary devices, sentence structure and word choice to manipulate the mood, meaning and purpose of the text.
- To compare and contrast fiction and nonfiction.

### Essential Questions:

- How are fiction and nonfiction similar?
- How are fiction and nonfiction different?

## Planning

### Long-term Planning

Table 5.1 shows how the lesson fits into the yearly planning. The lesson falls within Unit 4 where the topic is Fiction and Nonfiction. The yearly long-term planning is designed to cover all six state Standard units in ELA before the state testing in early March. The Text Task (TT) covered

*Table 5.1* Long-term Planning

| Weeks | ELA |
|-------|-----|
| 1–4 | Unit 1—Vocabulary/Fluency |
| 5–7 | Unit 2—Speaking & Listening |
| 8–13 | Unit 3—Comprehension |
| 14–17 | Unit 4—Fiction/Nonfiction |
| 18–22 | Unit 5—Writing Process |
| 23–27 | Unit 6—Types of Writing |
| 28–32 | Unit 7—Real World ELA |
| 33–38 | Unit 8—Technology in ELA |

in the lesson is Number 32, which is for the students to use a graphic organizer to compare and contrast the text structures of fiction and nonfiction texts.

### ELA Access Points

- LAFS.4.RI.2.AP.5b—Identify the specific structure (e.g., chronology, comparison, cause/effect and problem/solution) of events, ideas, concepts or information in a text excerpt.
- LAFS.5.RI.2.AP.5d—Compare and contrast the overall structure (e.g., chronology, comparison, cause/effect and problem/solution) of events, ideas, concepts or information in two or more texts.
- LAFS.6.RI.1.AP.1a—Use textual evidence to support inferences.
- LAFS.7.RI.1.AP.1a—Use two or more pieces of evidence to support inferences, conclusions or summaries of text.
- LAFS.8.RI.1.AP.1a—Use two or more pieces of evidence to support inferences, conclusions or summaries of text.

### Medium-term Planning

The medium-term planning can be found in Table 5.2 and shows that this lesson fits within Unit 4.

### Short-term Planning

The short-term planning is demonstrated in Table 5.3 and shows this lesson spanned over 1 week.

*Table 5.2* Medium-term Planning

| | Unit 4 | Assignments |
|---|---|---|
| November 30–<br>January 4 | *Fiction/Nonfiction*<br><br>**OVERVIEW**: Students will explore the differences between fiction and nonfiction. They will compare and contrast different genres and their literary devices.<br><br>**Essential Understanding: (Concrete)**<br>Students will be able to identify symbols of poetry.<br><br>Students will be able to identify a literary device.<br><br>Students will be able to build grade-appropriate vocabulary using strategies including context clues and study of word parts.<br><br>**Essential Understanding: (Representation)**<br>Students will analyze how authors use literary devices, sentence structure and word choice to manipulate the mood, meaning and purpose of the text.<br><br>Students will be able to compare and contrast fiction and nonfiction.<br><br>Students will be able to make their own selection of a text.<br><br>Students will be able to determine differences between historical fiction and nonfiction.<br><br>**Essential Questions:**<br>How are fiction and nonfiction similar?<br><br>How are fiction and nonfiction different? | **Text Task 20a**: After reading a **fiction** text, create a circle map to define the text type using text characteristics.<br><br>**Text Task 20b**: After reading a **nonfiction** text, create a circle map to define the text type using text characteristics.<br><br>**Text Task 32**: Use a graphic organizer to compare and contrast the text structures of **fiction and nonfiction texts**.<br><br>**Text Task 34**: **After reading a text**, complete a graphic organizer constructing the sequence of events. |

*Table 5.3* Short-term Planning

| Day | Activity |
|---|---|
| Monday | Review Scale with learning objectives. Read *Elmer* and discuss "wh" questions. |
| Tuesday | Discuss text structures of *Elmer* (fiction book). |
| Wednesday | Read *From Egg to Adult: The Life Cycle of Mammals* (pages related to elephants). Discuss text structures of a nonfiction book. |
| Thursday | Review text features of fiction and nonfiction and complete graphic organizer with visual supports. |
| Friday | Compare completed graphic organizer to scale to self-assess level of performance. |

## Progress Scale

Scales are used to track student progress for the entire week, not just for one lesson. The learning goal is always Level Three, so that there is always room for a Level Four assignment, which makes sure that even the higher level students are challenged. At the beginning of this particular lesson, the students were at Level One. Table 5.4 illustrates the Progress Chart used for this lesson.

Table 5.5 demonstrates how the personalized targets of the students were naturally integrated into the lesson. This shows that throughout the lesson, Mrs. T. was able to meet the personal targets of the students in an enhanced curriculum standards-referenced lesson.

## The Lesson: Fact or Fiction

The students were very familiar with using a four-level scale that builds on simple tasks to achieve the learning objective. The same process for assessment is used in all academic subjects so it seems easier for the student to focus on a new concept when they are accustomed to the development of the lesson. The students were able to categorize the different text structures when they had the visual support of cards and books to view. Without the visual supports, Mrs. T. felt the lesson would not have been as successful.

### Learning Goal

The learning goal on the scale is used for the weekly grading rubric also. Points are added to the rubric for work completion and student engagement. Each level of the scale has specific discrete tasks for the

*Table 5.4* Progress Chart

*Grade:* K-12 *Subject:* ELA *Unit #4 TT#:* 32 *EU* Students will be able to compare and contrast fiction and nonfiction. *Unit Title:* Fiction/Nonfiction Week # 16

*Standards:* (LAFS.3.RI.3.AP.8a; LAFS.4.RI.2.AP.5b; LAFS.5.RI.2.AP.5d; LAFS.6.RI.1.AP.1c; LAFS.7.RI.1.AP.1a; LAFS.8.RI.1.AP.1a)

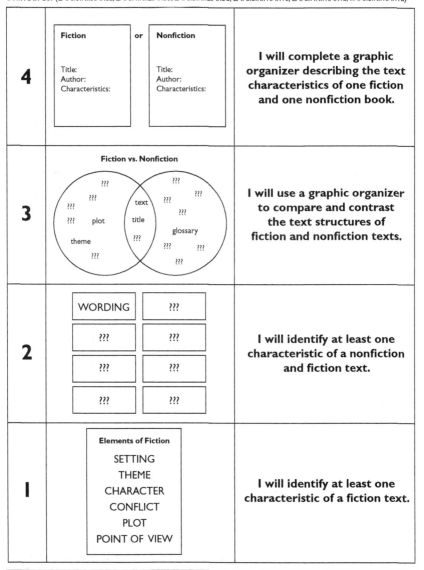

| | | |
|---|---|---|
| **4** | Fiction or Nonfiction — Title: Author: Characteristics: / Title: Author: Characteristics: | **I will complete a graphic organizer describing the text characteristics of one fiction and one nonfiction book.** |
| **3** | Fiction vs. Nonfiction — ??? plot theme ??? / text title glossary ??? | **I will use a graphic organizer to compare and contrast the text structures of fiction and nonfiction texts.** |
| **2** | WORDING ??? / ??? ??? / ??? ??? / ??? ??? | **I will identify at least one characteristic of a nonfiction and fiction text.** |
| **1** | Elements of Fiction — SETTING THEME CHARACTER CONFLICT PLOT POINT OF VIEW | **I will identify at least one characteristic of a fiction text.** |

*Table 5.5* Personal Target Engagement

| Student | Targets | Review |
|---------|---------|--------|
| Krystal | To respond to "Wh" questions, "Who," "What," "Where" and "When", accurately. | Krystal needed the extra visual supports of text features and gestures to respond correctly to "What story is fiction and why?" but she was able to determine with several trials. |
| | To identify numbers 1–10. | Krystal located the page numbers in the story to reinforce number identification. |
| | To take turns and increase tolerance time for non-preferred teacher-directed tasks. | During the lesson, Krystal practiced wait time by going second or third in her small group to complete a section of the activity. |
| Calvin | To answer "Wh" questions and use the text for reference. | Calvin used the nonfiction text to locate the "Table of context and index section" to respond to "How can we identify the text?" |
| | To complete one-to-one correspondence. | Calvin counted all the text features he located at the end of the session successfully. |
| | To increase independent time on task (4 minutes). | Calvin searched for text clues for about 2½ minutes when the book was placed in his possession with adult modeling. |
| Kaley | To respond to "Why" questions in reading comprehension. | Kaley worked on this goal by supporting her answer with "Elmer was a nonfiction book because the story was fake and the pictures were not real." |
| | To express her emotions peacefully. | Kaley was able to minimize her calling out when she was consistently re-directed to focus on one of the text features. |
| Joaquin | To use a preferred mode of communication to identify and describe key details independently. | Joaquin used his TouchChat to locate "elephant" and "fiction." He also slid the correct visuals to their respective column on his folder. |
| | To raise his right hand to get the teacher's attention independently. | Joaquin raised his hand when class was asked who wanted a break after completing their work. Although this action was not completely independent it is a natural prompt to increase the desired behavior. |

| | | |
|---|---|---|
| Jarrett | To use text to respond to questions and add more details in his responses. | Jarrett supported his responses by finding "Text captions," "Tell about the picture," "Table of Contents" and "Pages" on the nonfiction text. |
| | To attempt and complete work with fewer verbal outbursts of "Too much" and to ask for assistance in a calmer tone with no more than one verbal cue. | Jarrett said "I am done" but tolerated redirection without a louder burst when asked to create a fictional text. |
| Robert | To ask questions of peers using strategies. To maximize speech intelligibility, such as sound approximations, slow rate and eye contact. | Robert asked Kaley "Are talking animals real?" when teacher directed in small groups and made eye contact with him. |
| | To increase his self-advocacy skills. | During the session, Robert was prompted "What do you need to complete work?" and Robert responded "I need glue." |
| Rafael | To spontaneously use his communication device to: a) request objects or activities, b) greet adults/peers. To identify all the letters of his first name and input them into his communication device. | Rafael used his TouchChat to describe Elmer as "different," and "colors." Rafael spelled his first name on TouchChat to instruct teacher how to write on his assignment. He spelled "Ramno." |
| | To demonstrate the values of 1–10. | Rafael counted all the text characteristics he had on his folder using his TouchChat. |
| Niabi | To use six picture symbols representing language concepts (i.e., hot, cold, dirty, clean, on, off). To describe photographs independently. To match two words that are the same using visual or verbal cues. To use a keyboard to correctly type a given word. | Niabi located "colors," "elephant" and "jungle" on her TouchChat. She typed her name on TouchChat when given one letter at a time. |
| | To increase task time and reduce frequency of getting up from seat to search for sensory input. | Niabi gathered all materials (glue and scissors) and passed out to students, which allowed her to remain on task when she sat down to complete work. |

students to complete in order to progress through the scale. Each student is exposed to the learning goal, although some students may not reach mastery of the objective. Jarrett and Kaley reached a Level Four with verbal directions and few picture supports. Joaquin and Robert reached a Level Three by sliding answers to the correct location. Joaquin responded with his personal iPad and Robert supported his answers verbally. Rafael required visual supports and multiple trials to complete his responses. His hands shake consistently so using his communication device takes extra time. Calvin reached a Level Three with extra time and repetition to process information due to being easily distracted. Niabi and Krystal reached a Level Three with multiple adult modeling trials.

## Other Skills

### Fundamental ELA Skills

Mrs. T. began the lesson by asking wondering questions that the student had to think about: "I wonder what this book is about?" "I wonder if this book is fiction or nonfiction?" "How can I tell?" "Who is the author?" "Who is the illustrator?" These were all recursive skills that are naturally embedded into the lesson.

Social skills were also incorporated to make connections with how people that look physically different, like Elmer did in the story, should be treated. Mrs. T. facilitated a conversation about how Calvin looks different now with his compression garments covering his torso and left hand, yet he is still the same. Connections were explicitly made with the Elmer story.

## Student Engagement

The students are very familiar with the instructional process of scale/ learning goals introduction, whole group story time, whole group interactive questions and answers with the use of low-tech (visuals) and high-tech (Mimio, iPads and interactive communication boards) followed by small group task time. At the completion of their tasks the students get a 10-minute break where they are allowed to choose a preferred center. When the lesson involves discussion about their personal lives they are more engaged, such as this lesson. When student engagement diminishes, Mrs. T. employs high interest tangibles to increase interest so that the students can complete a lesson with purposeful learning. In this lesson, that strategy was not needed. There were also many visuals for students to look at and touch that provided extra sensory support.

## Reasons Mrs. T. Believes This Was an Effective Lesson (This Section is Written in the First Person)

The lesson went well overall. The students are very familiar with using a four-level Progress Scale that builds on simple tasks to achieve the learning objective. The same process for assessment is used in all academic subjects so it seems easier for the students to focus on a new concept when they are accustomed to the structure of the lesson. The students were able to categorize the different text structures when they had the visual support of cards and books to view. Without the visual supports or sensory rich supports, I feel the lesson would not have been as successful.

The lessons are built around Universal Design for Learning (UDL) concepts. Therefore, students are given the resources to represent and express their knowledge through their specific mode of communication. Lessons are also dynamic to increase student engagement. These are systems that are embedded into lesson planning explicitly supported through the schools' Professional Learning Communities (PLCs). I feel that the strategies that are employed across Orchard Hill are very effective due to the rich discussions and teacher collaborations that occur prior to building lessons. These group discussions increase possible strategies to use within lessons that expand the teachers' own comfort level.

The lesson included the use of Graphic Organizers, which allowed the students to represent their learning in a non-linguistic way. The structure of the Visual Organizer helped the students examine similarities and differences, and I used this throughout instruction to define or negate concepts. The lesson included activities where students had to support their answers with text evidence, which I believe builds lifelong learning skills. Lastly, the students were given opportunities throughout the lesson to self-evaluate with the academic Progress Scale and performance checks.

Repetition and activities that involve motor skills appear to increase my students' engagement regardless of motor ability. Pairing fiction and nonfiction picture books that are based on student interests has also positively impacted student achievement. My students love animals so I make a conscious effort to incorporate animals into the lessons. Flexible grouping that adjusts to students' daily needs is not always easy but, when this occurs, the lesson outcomes have been more successful. For this lesson, it was more effective to work 1:2 (teacher/student ratio) instead of our normal 1:3. Also, using pictures and/or photos that were lesson specific helped my students make connections with text structure.

# Chapter 6

# Hatchet

*With Lora Reese*

This lesson takes place at Spring Park School in a class in the DAT team.

## The Classroom

The classroom consists of seven students in total. Six students use customized wheelchairs and one student moves around the room independently. This Developmental Assistive Technology (DAT) classroom is multi-grade to include sixth, seventh, eighth and ninth graders. The students access learning through the use of varying levels of Assistive Technology (AT). A myriad of low to high Assistive Technology choices are available for the students, such as varying forms of Alternative Augmentative Communication (AAC), Pragmatic Organization Dynamic Display (PODD), picture displays and other adaptive devices. The teacher provides a balance of direct instruction and small group activities with consistent paraprofessional support. The classroom follows a Spring Park created planning, which is aligned to the state Standard Access Points. The materials selected or created for the academic lessons are based on these Access Points.

## The Adults

The staff includes one teacher and two paraprofessionals with integrated therapeutic services provided through an on-campus team who include a physical therapist, occupational therapist, speech and language pathologist and a Local Assistive Technology Service (LATS) team. Ms. L. is certified in Exceptional Student Education (ESE) and Elementary Education K–12 with an English Speaking Other Language (ESOL) endorsement. In 2003, Ms. L. left the world of business in software development to begin her journey in special education. She served 4 years as a one-on-one paraprofessional supporting middle-school students with Autism Spectrum Disorder (ASD) and 4 years aiding elementary and middle-school students with Emotional Behavior Disorder (EBD). Since the inception of her career, she has obtained a Bachelor of Science in Elementary Education and a Master of Arts in Exceptional Student Education. The support staff includes paraprofessional Ms. K., who is a former Home Economics teacher, and Ms. D., who is a former licensed massage therapist with prior experience in childcare.

## The Students

JC, a delightful 11-year-old, is a young man with emerging language. He is identified under the disability categories of Traumatic Brain Injury (TBI) and Speech or Language Impairment (SLI) and receives the services of occupational therapy, physical therapy and speech and language therapy. He receives therapies out of the classroom with follow-up support provided by the teacher and paraprofessionals in the classroom. JC eats pureed food, which is fed to him by an adult, and requires full adult assistance for transition and personal needs. He is able to nod or smile to encourage his peers, and take turns during conversations and classroom game time, which he does by holding his head away from his head switches. He demonstrates understanding of basic number, color and shape recognition. JC accurately identifies the days of the week in order, significant dates on the calendar, demonstrates understanding of common signs in the world around him (stop, go, warning, hot, cold) and communicates his feelings of displeasure as well as making requests through minimal verbalizations, but mostly through the use of a dedicated AAC device, which is an iPad. He communicates his desired goals through the use of this dedicated AAC device and indicates that he wants to have a job where he can be a cook because he likes to eat. For fun, JC likes to watch movies. When asked what he wants to learn how to do, he responds with "Bus driver."

His Daily Instructional Goals (emerging from his IEP) are:

- To use a two-switch interface with a dedicated AAC device equipped with customized communication software to respond correctly to comprehension questions in five out of five routines.
- To engage in socialization activities and game playing routines with his peers by following simple one-step rules and waiting his turn in five out of five routines.

MD, a joyful 15-year-old, is a young lady with emerging language. She is identified under the disability categories of Orthopedic Impairment (OI) and Speech or Language Impairment (SLI) and receives the services of occupational therapy and physical therapy. MD receives therapies out of the classroom with follow-up support provided by the teacher and paraprofessionals in the classroom. She is on a continuous feeding (G-tube and J-tube) system, is seizure prone and requires full adult assistance for all personal care. She is able to use basic American Sign Language (ASL) to answer general "Yes/No" questions and sign "OK," or she makes a clicking sound with her tongue when she agrees with something. MD points to objects she desires and easily identifies adults and peers that she knows well. She demonstrates an understanding of basic number, color and shape recognition by using her dominant hand to point to or sort objects, or through the use of her AAC, which is her personal iPad with customized Proloquo2Go boards. She gestures when she wants something, laughs aloud when adults act silly and communicates when she does not feel well with ASL and her personal AAC. She is motivated by one-on-one attention that is entertaining and fun, will avoid tasks that do not interest her and dislikes loud noises. She uses her iPad and picture symbols to indicate her long-term transition goals when presented with a transition planning inventory worksheet. MD shared through a picture symbol transition planning sheet about vocational opportunities that she prefers to work in a clean environment that is inside where she can work on the same task at a slow pace while sitting and working with adults she knows. She wants to ride a bike, go camping, learn to grow a garden, learn to read better and go dancing. She plans to continue living with her family and hopes to learn budgeting skills, use kitchen appliances, cook, do laundry and choose her own clothing to wear. MD enjoys amusement parks, watching TV and movies, shopping, visiting friends and going out to eat with her family.

Her Daily Instructional Goals (emerging from her IEP) are:

- To use a dedicated AAC touch screen device equipped with customized communication software to respond correctly to comprehension questions related to a short story or word problem in two of three attempts, given a choice set of three, independently.
- To greet her friends in class and practice taking turns participating in a "Say it, spell it, say it" vocabulary word exercise. She uses her personal iPad with customized boards to say "Hi" to her classmates by name and to indicate if a student is not present or prompt them for their turn during game time. She uses the keyboard function on her iPad to spell vocabulary words and "say" the words in turn with her classmates in three out of five routines.

SK, a wonderful 13-year-old, is a young man with emerging language. He is identified under the disability categories of Intellectual Disability (InD), Speech or Language Impairment (SLI), Autism Spectrum Disorder (ASD) and is seizure prone. SK receives no specialized therapy outside of the classroom environment. He eats pureed food, which is fed to him by an adult, and requires full adult assistance to navigate his world and meet his personal needs. He makes direct eye contact when he is spoken to. However, he struggles with visual attendance to academic and social activities. SK smiles and makes joyful utterances when he is happy. He indicates, through pictorial symbols, when presented with a transition planning worksheet, that he would like to work in a clean environment that is inside where he can work on the same task at a slow pace while sitting and working alone. He would like to remain living at home with family where he can help his mom cook, do laundry and learn to use kitchen appliances. SK enjoys watching movies, listening to music and spending time with his family.

His Daily Instructional Goals (emerging from his IEP) are:

- To demonstrate unit vocabulary recognition and answer comprehension questions in four out of five trials by using an eye gaze or hand-over-hand.
- To greet his friends in class and practice turn taking while participating in the vocabulary words exercise in the morning routine through the use of AAC and eye gaze select in four out of five trials as measured by teacher observation.

KD, a sweet and animated 14-year-old, is a young lady with emerging language. She is identified under the disability categories of Intellectual Disability (InD) and Speech or Language Impairment (SLI). KD receives physical therapy out of the classroom with follow-up support provided by the teacher and paraprofessionals in the classroom. She eats regular food that is pureed from home and she is seizure prone. She requires full adult assistance in transitioning from activity to activity and meeting her personal needs. She will crawl around the room when given the opportunity at home and school. However, she requires full support to stand. KD makes direct eye contact with adults and her peers. She recognizes her name and turns her head in the direction of the person who is talking to her. She occasionally smiles and often makes happy utterances. KD participates in her learning environment through the use of various low-tech and high-tech AAC devices including hand-over-hand support with communication books, an eye gaze system built out of PVC piping and Velcro dots to secure pictures and BIGmack switches for cause-and-effect activities. She communicates with her eyes, facial expressions and vocalizations. Through the use of pictorial symbols, she indicates that she enjoys reading and learning new skills in a clean environment where she can be with her friends. We have long-term plans to graduate her communication to a Pragmatic Organization Dynamic Display (PODD), to encourage more independent choice making as opposed to basic cause-and-effect and "Yes/No" responses.

Her Daily Instructional Goals (emerging from her IEP) are:

- To demonstrate core vocabulary recognition and answer comprehension questions in four out of five trials by using a BIGmack switch or direct picture selection.
- To greet her friends through the use of AAC in four out of five trials.

LP, a sweet 16-year-old, is a young lady with emerging language. She is identified under the disability categories of Intellectual Disability (InD) and Speech or Language Impairment (SLI) for which she receives therapeutic pull out for speech, which is then supported by the teacher and support staff in the classroom. LP is a delightfully happy young woman who laughs often and easily recognizes adults and peers she knows well. She eats regular food and drinks water from a cup with assistance. She is able to reach for and sort objects. LP requires full assistance to transition from place to place and to maintain her personal needs. She actively engages in learning and social opportunities with a verbal "yeah" response and shakes her head from side to side to indicate "no" while placing her hand up to show lack of interest. She indicates through the use of pictorial symbols, when presented with a transition planning worksheet, that she prefers to work in an active and clean environment where her efforts are supported with full assistance. She prefers to be with her mom or adult females she knows well and displays some interest in learning about clothing and fashion.

Her Daily Instructional Goals (emerging from her IEP) are:

- To demonstrate core vocabulary recognition by visually scanning pictures and words to answer comprehension questions in two out of three trials by using a BIGmack switch or direct picture selection.
- To greet her friends in class verbally by making direct eye contact and giving a high-five. She practices taking turns participating in Math games and number recognition activities through the use of AAC in two out of three trials.

DW, a happy 13-year-old, is a young man with emerging language. He is identified under the disability categories of Intellectual Disability (InD) and Orthopedic Impairment (OI). He is on consult with his therapy services, which is where the classroom staff follow advice from therapists during their everyday support of DW. He eats regular food provided from home, cut into bite-sized pieces, and additional nutritional supplements. He requires full adult assistance for positioning, movement and meeting personal needs. He will lift his head when adults say his name and ask him to engage in his academics by answering comprehension questions. He uses a small switch mounted with an adjustable arm on his wheelchair in a position that he is able to activate easily using his head. This adaptive switch has a cord that connects to almost any device in the room. While DW is unable to verbalize his desires with consistent responses, he maintains engagement by accessing his switch when he has something to contribute to the lesson or simply to gain the attention of staff. He finds it quite entertaining to activate a recorded switch frequently that says, "Ms. L., I have something to say," during a lesson, to which he smiles when responded to. Based on teacher observations of his behaviors, DW desires to be a part of the activities, to include answering questions regarding the lesson and to activate a switch to read to his peers. He demonstrates enjoyment by smiling and actively participating by lifting his head. He appears to like loud and silly noises and activities on the computer by smiling, lifting his hand to his mouth while making joyful sounds, and lifting his head to make direct eye contact with adults or to look directly at the activity.

His Daily Instructional Goals (emerging from his IEP) are:

• To use his head to activate a switch to read a story to his peers and make single choice selections within five physical prompts.
• To respond by raising his head and opening his eyes.

KM is an active, ambulatory 13-year-old young man with emerging language. He is identified under the disability categories of Intellectual Disability (InD) and Speech or Language Impairment (SLI). KM receives therapeutic pull out for speech and language therapy services once a week as well as push in once weekly. He has visual and physical challenges, which creates problems as he navigates his environment. He eats pureed food independently and meets his personal needs with adult prompting. He provides verbal responses with some clarity in enunciation. He uses personalized AAC to communicate in the classroom, including a classroom iPad, low- and high-tech assistive technology, adaptive switches and communication boards with words supporting picture symbols.

Through the use of pictorial symbols, when presented with a transition planning worksheet with supporting words, KM directly selects and verbalizes that he prefers to work in a clean environment that is inside where he can work on the same task at a slow pace while sitting and working alone. He prefers to be told how to do things and requires help following a schedule for starting and completing work on time. He is able to ask for help if needed. He enjoys playing the drums, going camping and wants to learn to do better in Math. KM likes watching TV, listening to music and going on vacation with his family.

His Daily Instructional Goals (emerging from his IEP) are:

• To select an answer by touching the ActivBoard or a printed picture when answering comprehension questions related to a short story or word problem in three of four attempts, given a choice set of three, independently.
• To use assistive technology, verbal communication or picture cues to state his preferences in four of five attempts.

## Overview of Lesson

The literacy lesson is based on the book *Hatchet*, by Gary Paulsen (1987). This age-appropriate Newbery Honor winning story is the first in a series of five books authored by Gary Paulsen. A young adolescent boy, Brian, is being sent to visit his father in Canada when the small airplane he is traveling in with a single pilot does not make it safely to the destination. Brian is forced to learn important survival skills while he is lost in the Canadian wilderness for nearly 2 months. A gift of a hatchet was given to Brian for his trip, which he used to make fire, a bow, arrows and a spear. Over the days, Brian has many exciting and frightening experiences.

The story was chosen to offer adventure opportunities to this dynamic group of adolescent learners. A select few of Brian's experiences are brought to life for the students as they listen to the story and create some of the survival items he used to make it through 54 days in the deep, dark, lonely woods of Canada. In the lesson the students collect sticks to make fishing poles with yarn and attach a magnet to the end. They then use the adapted fishing pole to "catch" a fish in a homemade pond using a paper clip on the fish. Next, the students choose the appropriate animals read about in the story, using an eye gaze system built by the teacher. Finally, picture symbols are used to complete a KWL chart (what you Know, what you Want to know and what you want to Learn) to build sentences that become a personalized paragraph by each student to demonstrate their connection to the story. These activities support independent functioning through choice-making opportunities, while reinforcing reading comprehension and literacy skills.

## Lesson Learning Goal

The vocabulary focused upon in the lesson, which Ms. L. intends the students to engage with, is:

- Birchbark
- Abating
- Altimeter
- Depress
- Transmissions
- Fuselage
- Stymied
- Copilot
- Flue
- Embedded

The lesson covers curriculum and learning areas including language arts, reading comprehension and literacy skills, in addition to providing opportunities to enhance social emotional growth during campus nature walks to gather supplies for outlined activities.

## Planning

### Long-term Planning

The long-term planning includes differentiated tasks to support the multiple levels and ages of the learners. The specific aspects of the long-term planning this lesson relates to are illustrated in Table 6.1, Leveled Differentiated Skills in Modified Curriculum at Spring Park School.

Table 6.1 Leveled Differentiated Skills in Modified Curriculum at Spring Park School

| Independently Functioning Students will... | Supported Students will... | Participatory Students will... |
| --- | --- | --- |
| • Using sentence strips, create a simple paragraph that includes a topic sentence, supporting facts and details and a concluding sentence.<br>• Demonstrate conventions of grammar in spoken and written sentence forms using recordable devices provided by teacher and staff.<br>• Demonstrate conventions of written language, including appropriate capitalization, end punctuation and common spelling, using activities on the interactive board to model by the teacher.<br>• Share information, ask and answer questions and make comments during a group discussion, using recordable devices with a minimum of three options. | • Select pictures with text to create a written document of factual sentences on a topic.<br>• Identify beginning capital letters and end punctuation in a written sentence.<br>• Spell familiar words with letter-sound matches.<br>• Use picture supports to share information, ask and answer questions and make comments during group discussions. | • Given errorless choices of pictures, make a selection to communicate facts on a given topic.<br>• With picture supports, combine two or more words during a shared writing or speaking activity.<br>• Locate capital letters and end punctuation in a sentence.<br>• Participate in conversational exchanges, using communication technology and picture supports. |

The standards this lesson references are:

- *Standards for Writing*—Text Types and Purposes: Generate a simple informative paragraph that includes a defined topic, supporting details and a concluding sentence.
- *Standards for Language*—Use conventions of grammar when speaking or writing. Use correct capitalization, punctuation and spelling in sentences.
- *Standards for Speaking and Listening*—Engage in grade level and age-appropriate discussions, including ability to follow rules of discussion and ask questions related to topics, respond to others' questions, make comments and share ideas.
- *Language Arts Access Point*—The specific ELA access point the lesson relates to is LAFS.11-12.RI.2.AP.6c.

### Medium-term Planning

The medium-term planning relates to chapter summary paragraphs as illustrated in Table 6.2, Medium-term Planning Learning Opportunities at Spring Park School.

### Short-term Planning

The short-term planning is illustrated in Table 6.3 and shows how this lesson spans across a week.

*Table 6.2* Medium-term Planning Learning Opportunities at Spring Park School

| Topic: Chapter Summary Paragraph, Using Unique Learning Systems Adapted Curriculum based on Florida Access Points | | | |
|---|---|---|---|
| Curriculum and Learning | Objectives | Activities | Assessment |
| LAFS.6.RL.2.4 Determine the meaning of words and phrases as they are used in a text, including figurative (e.g., metaphors, similes and idioms) and connotative meanings; analyze the impact of a specific word choice on meaning and tone. | Use context clues and illustrations to determine meanings of words and phrases in a text, including figurative meanings. Identify the structure of sentences, chapters or scenes that contributes to meaning of the text. | Students will identify a named picture related to the text from a single option or errorless choice. Students will identify a picture representing an event from a chapter or scene. | Use communication boards to capture student responses to the activity: Like it, Don't Like it, Want to do it again, Don't want to do it again. |

Table 6.3 Short-term Planning

| Day | Objective |
| --- | --- |
| Monday | Read Chapter 1 of *Hatchet*. |
| Tuesday | Read Chapter 2 of *Hatchet*.<br>Summarizing Text. |
| Wednesday | Read Chapter 3 of *Hatchet*.<br>Number Operations Adding and Subtracting. |
| Thursday | Read Chapter 4 of *Hatchet*.<br>Science Through Measurement and Math Concepts. |
| Friday | Read Chapter 5 of *Hatchet*.<br>Review and Assess. |

## The Lesson: *Hatchet*

The whole lesson takes place over a period of 3 weeks. The first week is shared here. The initial lesson includes the book introduction by the teacher with relevant real-world experiences shared to support text-to-self connections. Internet searches are performed to display pictures of various survival items to the students (hatchet, bow and arrows, fire starters, twine, etc.) to support text-to-world connections. The cover page with title and author is shown and explained. Each day a single chapter is read, beginning with a summary of the previous chapter events. Visual aids such as hands-on survival items are used to support an authentic experience for the learners to provide text-to-self student connections. Survival guide books are used to make text-to-text connections, making this a well-rounded literacy lesson.

### Monday

#### Whole Group Vocabulary Activity

Vocabulary words from the story are displayed on the interactive board (birchbark, abating, altimeter, depress, transmissions, fuselage, stymied, copilot, flue, embedded). Ms. L. defines each word using a sentence and real-world examples. For example, after a photo of each vocabulary word has been searched for, Ms. L. opens a word processing program with an existing word bank to create a sentence using one of the vocabulary words, "The *copilot* helps the pilot fly the plane." Each word has a picture symbol to assist in recognition for the students.

## Individual Vocabulary Activity

Each student spells the words using their respective AAC. The iPad users are equipped with the two most commonly used communication software programs in the class, Proloquo2Go and TouchChat. Each student with an iPad spells or locates the word, then builds the same sentence that has been modeled on the board. Students with communication books locate each word accordingly to build the same sentence. Students who require more assistance activate a switch that reads the sentence on the board after choosing the correct picture from the eye gaze system. This activity is done for each vocabulary word highlighted from the text.

## Whole Group Activity

As a class, sentences are built using each vocabulary word previously chosen from the text. Ms. L. models building a sentence by explaining the five important components that make up a sentence (subject, predicate, clause, phrase and modifier) and a vocabulary word from the text. The paraprofessionals circulate through the group and support individual students as needed with their personal AAC to build a sentence using a chosen vocabulary word.

## Tuesday

### Whole Group KWL Activity

This is an opportunity to assess the students' comprehension of the text. A KWL chart is used to look specifically at the animals in the story and how they impact Brian's survival on the island. Ms. L. places a blank KWL chart under the document camera to project onto the interactive board to explain the activity to the students. Figure 6.1 illustrates the chart.

Research is begun to complete the KWL chart by having each student choose one animal from the story that they recognize using the teacher-designed eye gaze system. The type of food the animal eats and environments where the animal commonly lives are then researched. This activity is completed by using the Internet and various books from the library and classroom. Figure 6.2 illustrates MD engaged in this activity.

### Individual KWL Activity

Each student comes up to the interactive board to locate a picture of the animal they chose and match it to the word. For example, KM chooses the picture of a porcupine and then finds the word "porcupine" on the board to drag to the picture (Figure 6.3). Ms. L. has KM mimic her spelling his

| K-W-L | | | |
|---|---|---|---|
| | **What I know** | **What I want to know** | **What I learned** |
| **KD** |  | What do bears eat? | Bears eat berries and fish. |
| **KM** |  | What do porcupines eat? | Porcupines eat tree bark. |
| **SM** |  | What do wolves eat? | Wolves eat small animals. |
| **MD** |  | What do moose eat? | Moose eat plants and berries. |
| **LP** |  | What do fish eat? | Fish eat small fish. |
| **DW** |  | What do skunks eat? | Skunks eat fish, berries and insects. |
| **JC** |  | What does Brian eat? | Brian eats berries and fish. |

Figure 6.1 KWL chart.

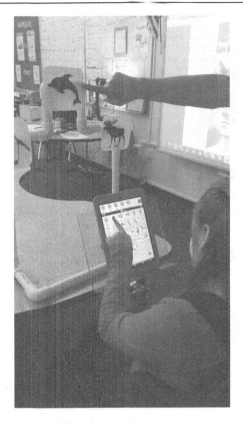

*Figure 6.2* MD using her personal iPad to select the correct animal being discussed as Ms. K. points to each of the animal photos on the eye gaze system.

chosen word. Some students require hand-over-hand support and recordable switches to complete this exercise while others do this independently.

### Whole Group Activity

To continue making connections, a sentence is read from the text where each animal plays a role and impacts Brian's survival. For example, as Brian comes across a moose, he is suddenly struck with fear, as her great size that he only knows from pictures is suddenly quite real. The moose attacks Brian multiple times by ramming into his body, driving him into the muddy bank of the lake. Every time he moves, she charges again. He finally learns that if he moves very slowly, only a foot at a time on his hands and knees, he can carefully creep to safety. Even though he is terribly injured, his will to survive is stronger than the pain as he moves.

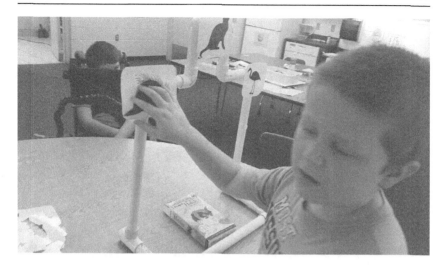

*Figure 6.3* KM is using a teacher-designed eye gaze system to select directly the animal he believes belongs in the sentence he is building.

As a class, a paragraph is constructed to summarize the key details learned about each of the animals and events in the story. Ms. L. models the creation of a paragraph. Then Ms. L. uses an iPad with TouchChat placed under the document camera for the students to mimic, creating a sentence each. The paraprofessionals support individual students as needed with their personal form of communication.

## Wednesday

### Whole Group Sentence Activity

Ms. L. models, using correct punctuation to create individual sentences from the student created KWL chart, as what has been learned about what the animals in the story eat is revisited.

### Individual Sentence Activity

Each student's sentence is typed on the interactive board with various grammar and punctuation errors. The students use their own form of communication to identify and correct the errors. For example, JC will use his iPad and communication software to indicate the first word of the sentence needs to be a capital letter and then he will add the correct punctuation at the end. Incorrect sentence: "the black bear eats red berries?" Correct sentence: "The black bear eats red berries." Figure 6.4 illustrates JC using his iPad to correct a sentence.

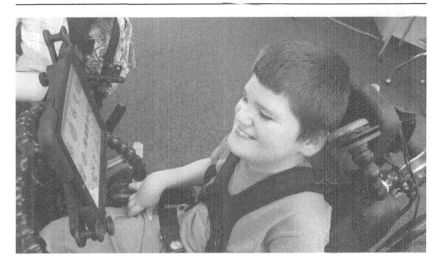

*Figure 6.4* JC using an iPad to correct a sentence.

### Whole Group Activity

As a class, a story is created using real-world relevant examples based on the animals the students studied from the story. Ms. L. models this on the classroom interactive board. The paraprofessionals circulate through the group and support individual students as needed.

### Thursday

#### Whole Group Hands-On Activity

Today, the group is going fishing. Ms. L. uses the document camera to model how to assemble a fishing pole using a stick collected during an earlier nature walk with a piece of yarn and a magnet. The steps to catching a fish are described using the PBS video, "Wild Kratts: Bass Class," and Ms. L. shares her real-world experiences as she grew up fishing using her own fishing pole and tackle.

#### Individual Hands-On Activity

Each student then follows a step-by-step plan to set up their fishing pole. First they choose the color of string they wish to use to make their fishing pole and assemble it with support. They tie a magnet to the end of their fishing line to resemble a hook and bait, and finally they practice casting their line into the man-made pond, constructed using a box with blue and green tissue paper. Figure 6.5 shows LP fishing with a pole she has made.

*Figure 6.5* LP is using the fishing pole she made to catch a fish using a paper clip and a small magnet.

## Whole Group Activity

Students take turns "catching" a fish made from tissue paper from the pond. Reference to the text is emphasized by Ms. L. For example, in the story Brian made other survival items with the hatchet given to him by his mother, such as a spear to hunt and capture his food.

## Friday

### Whole Group Storyboard Activity

Storyboards are created at the end of each week of reading the book. Students choose from three pictures, which describe events that occur throughout the book. Each picture includes key details from throughout the text. The students have to determine which picture describes what they have read. Two out of the three picture choices provided include future

*Table 6.4* Personal Target Engagement

| Student | Targets | Review |
|---------|---------|--------|
| JC | To use a two-switch interface with a dedicated AAC device equipped with customized communication software to respond correctly to comprehension questions in five out of five routines. | JC used his iPad to respond to a question about what animals were in the story *Hatchet*. |
| | To engage in socialization activities and game playing routines with his peers by following simple one-step rules and waiting his turn in five out of five routines. | Supported with hand-over-hand prompting, JC was successful in following the four-step plan for assembling the fishing pole and catching a fish. |
| | | JC waited his turn for adult support during the fishing activity. |
| MD | To use a dedicated AAC touch screen device equipped with customized communication software to respond correctly to comprehension questions related to a short story or word problem. | MD used her iPad to respond to the question about what animals were in the story *Hatchet*. |
| | To greet her friends in class and practice taking turns participating in a "Say it, spell it, say it" vocabulary word exercise. She uses her personal iPad with customized boards to say "Hi" to her classmates by name and to indicate if a student is not present or prompt them for their turn during game time. She uses the keyboard function on her iPad to spell vocabulary words and "say" the words in turn with her classmates in three out of five routines. | MD followed a model to spell each vocabulary word using her iPad (birchbark, abating, altimeter, depress, transmissions, fuselage, stymied, copilot, flue, embedded). Once each word was spelled, MD pressed the Proloquo2Go symbol for the words to be audibly expressed. |
| SK | To demonstrate unit vocabulary recognition and answer comprehension questions in four out of five trials by using eye gaze or hand-over-hand. | In response to what animals are in the story, an adult physically moved SK's hand to the correct picture on the eye gaze system. He then looked at the picture of the animal where his hand was pointing. |
| | To greet his friends in class and practice turn taking while participating in the vocabulary words exercise in the morning routine through the use of AAC and eye gaze select in four out of five trials. | During the morning vocabulary exercise, SK looked in the direction of each of his friends when the adult said their name and stood behind the student. |

| | | |
|---|---|---|
| KD | To demonstrate core vocabulary recognition and answer comprehension questions in four out of five trials by using a BIGmack switch or direct picture selection. | Once a picture was presented on the interactive board, KD would use her hand to choose one of the two recorded switches to match the picture to the audio of the vocabulary word. |
| | To greet her friends through the use of an assistive technology and direct select in four out of five trials. | Not addressed in this lesson. |
| LP | To demonstrate core vocabulary recognition by visually scanning pictures and words to answer comprehension questions in two out of three trials by using a BIGmack switch or direct picture selection. | LP looked directly at the interactive board with three pictures where one represented a vocabulary word from the story. When verbally prompted to find the picture, LP visually scanned the board and touched the correct picture matching the vocabulary word. |
| | To greet her friends in class verbally by making direct eye contact and giving a high-five. To practice taking turns participating in Math games and number recognition activities through the use of AAC devices and direct select in two out of three trials. | During the lesson, LP "high-fived" her peers as they answered the comprehension questions related to the story Hatchet. |
| DW | To use his head to activate a switch to read a story to his peers and make single choice selections within five physical prompts. | DW used his head to activate a switch with a recorded sentence from the story Hatchet. |
| | To respond by raising his head and opening his eyes. | DW raised his head and looked at the adult each time a vocabulary word from the story was spoken. |
| KM | To select an answer by touching the ActivBoard or a printed picture when answering comprehension questions related to a short story or word problem in three of four attempts, given a choice set of three, independently. | KM walked up to the class interactive board to correctly select the picture in response to a comprehension question from events in the story Hatchet. For example, the adult would ask what vehicle the character in the story traveled in when visiting his father. |
| | To use assistive technology, verbal communication or picture cues to state his preferences in four of five school days. | During the fishing pole activity, KM indicated his preference of color and bait for catching a fish in the pond made with the class. |

events that take place in the story. Using this method supports comprehension as well as the opportunity to make predictions of what the students think is going to happen next. For the first story board, the students are shown a picture of a plane, a picture of a bus and a picture of a train. Once each student chooses the plane, the group discusses how Brian traveled in a small plane with just a pilot and then searches for pictures to create the first story board using Microsoft Word and the Internet. A search is made for pictures of a plane, a boy and a pilot. The students decide on the photos, which are printed and hung on the wall. This activity is continued throughout the remainder of the story. The culmination of storyboards provides a constant reminder of the story as it unfolds.

Table 6.4 demonstrates how the personalized targets of the students were naturally integrated into the lesson. This shows that, throughout the lesson, Ms. L. was able to meet the personal needs of the students in an enhanced curriculum standards-referenced lesson.

## Reasons Ms. L. Believes This Was an Effective Lesson (This Section is Written in the First Person)

In my classroom, I teach to the level where each student is presently learning. I feel it is important to recognize that this level can and will change by week or even day. It is my job, as a professional educator, to identify the present learning needs of my students at the time of each lesson. The students provide feedback through their emotions by smiling, laughing, even frowning with a look of confusion. They also use body language and their respective communication devices. It was apparent each day that the students were enthused with the lesson. Whether it was during the reading of the book *Hatchet* or the hands-on activities, the students were always engaged. MD and JC used their iPads to make random comments like "This is fun," or "Let me tell you something," indicating they wanted to share their feelings and the knowledge they were gaining. LP and KD often times clapped their hands or pounded on the table as they shrilled in happiness. KM particularly enjoyed assembling his fishing pole as he smiled hugely while working with Ms. D. SK and DW were the most engaged that I have ever seen, as they both struggle with excessive seizure activity most days. The two boys were awake, bobbing their heads, activating switches and making eye contact more often than usual. I believe the enthusiasm was contagious between the students and staff. The effectiveness of this lesson was demonstrated through the students' accuracy in recognizing the animals from the story and the consistent engagement. The excitement of the students has encouraged me to use this as a model for future lessons. The use of personal and classroom iPads with TouchChat, laminated pictures, the

Internet, communication books, picture books, the document camera, the eye gaze system and recordable switches equally supported a diverse learning environment as well as many unexpected teachable moments upon which to expound throughout the lesson.

The KWL chart served as a graphic organizer that supported a direct link to the text as we discussed what the students Know, Want to know and want to Learn about animals in the story. During this activity, I placed pictures of the animals in the story on the interactive board and asked the students to tell me something that describes an animal or an action or sound they make. JC used his head switches to activate his iPad with TouchChat to say, "Bears loud." MD used her iPad with Proloquo2Go to say, "Her mad." She said this when I pointed to the moose. After asking a few prompting questions, I determined that MD was referring to the part of the story where the moose and Brian had an unpleasant interaction. These are enormous connections for the students as they demonstrate comprehension on multiple levels while encouraging further discussions.

During our class discussions, I often shared stories of primitive camping trips I have taken with my family and friends. I explained to the students the importance of packing the necessary items for survival in the woods and the importance of having enough water. We talked about packing a knife for protection, a pot for boiling water for food, matches to start a fire, band-aids and other first-aid supplies, a tent and flashlight. I explained to the students why you should pack only what you know you need so your backpack is not overloaded for the long hike to the campsite. During these dialogs, the students made random on-topic comments and we always tied the details back to the main character. For example, when Brian made a raft and swam to the crashed airplane to obtain a survival kit and how he used his hatchet to punch a hole to enter the plane. This was the most exciting moment for me as a teacher because the students' facial expressions and comments made it quite apparent as their eyes lit up when we made those real-world to text connections. I knew they got it!

In an effort to bring the story to life, we took the students on a nature walk to collect sticks for our fishing poles while staff pointed out trees, bushes and the large lake behind the school. We explained to the students the types of animals commonly found in our area as we encouraged them to use adjectives to describe what they saw, heard or smelled.

Differentiating between direct instruction, shared readings between all three staff members and the use of various forms of assistive technology supported diverse learning opportunities for each student. Another pedagogical belief of mine is to encourage student-driven learning as much as possible. This is accomplished by always offering multiple choices to my students for every task. For example, I ask the students who they want to have read to them each day. A student chosen form of communication is another way to empower the students as their abilities vary. For example, some days a student who typically uses an iPad may choose to use a PODD as it allows them to gain support in developing their receptive or expressive language skills.

Overall, this was an effective lesson as students showed ongoing interest as they received instant feedback and validation during each activity from reading to making the fishing pole to building sentences with the vocabulary. The students received praise for being good listeners during reading, accolades for random comments they made and redirection when their responses were not relevant to the topic.

# Chapter 7

# Rhyming Literary Device— Green Eggs and Ham

*With David Hass*

This lesson takes place at Orchard Hill School.

## The Classroom

There are four students in the class, along with one teacher and two paraprofessionals. All of the students are on the state Standard Access Points, and all of them have Individualized Education Plans (IEPs). The students have mobility and fine motor issues. Three students are emerging communicators and one has limited verbal skills. All of the students have access to Alternative Augmentative Communication (AAC) devices. The students are taught in whole group, small group and individualized settings. The classroom follows an Orchard Hill created Scope and Sequence that is modified from the one the district uses, and aligned to the state Standard Access Points. The materials selected or created for the academic lessons are based on these Access Points, and not on a specific curriculum. All students come to school using individualized transportation.

## The Adults

Mr. D. is in his fifth year of teaching. He graduated with a Bachelor of Arts in Elementary Education in 2000. Mr. D. has taught in private Christian schools as well as in public education. When he entered the county he was a substitute teacher in all grade levels, then he became a paraprofessional at Orchard Hills. Shortly thereafter, Mr. D. was appointed a teacher at Orchard Hills where he spent his time in middle and high school classrooms. He received his English Speaking Other Language (ESOL) endorsement and Exceptional Student Education (ESE) certification in 2010.

Ms. E. has been a paraprofessional at Orchard Hills for a year and a half. Prior to that, she lived in Hall County, Georgia, where she worked as a teacher assistant in a preschool ESE department for 3 years. Ms. P. has been a paraprofessional for 8 years at Orchard Hills. She enjoys working with the students, as well as the staff.

## The Students

Suzanne uses simple one-press switches, paired with either pictures and/or words. Her primary exceptionality is Intellectual Disability (InD), but she also receives occupational therapy and physical therapy once a month. She also has a daily Nursing Care Plan. Her priority educational need is to develop her academic and life skills in order to become more independent. Suzanne is an emerging communicator and requires direct instruction with continuous hand-over-hand assistance to initiate and participate in daily activities. She has the ability to walk, but because she is not steady to walk alone, she uses a wheelchair.

Suzanne has four IEP goals: three for independent functioning, and one for communication. Her independent functioning goals are:

- To be able to sit at her work space without sweeping items off it.
- To press a switch to initiate an activity upon an adult directive.
- To place one item in a box with an adult directive and hand-over-hand assistance.

Her communication goal is:

- To choose between two different foods with verbal prompts.

Wilma is an emerging communicator, who raises her hand to indicate a need or a want and is able to feed herself. She moves around the classroom and school independently. Her primary exceptionality is Intellectual Disability (InD). She also has a daily Nursing Care Plan. When answering questions Wilma takes her time, looking closely at the text and/or item before pointing to her answer, sometimes needing physical prompting to respond. She enjoys coming to school and loves to match colors, shapes and pictures. Her priority educational need is to be able to express her needs and wants, as well as to become more independent.

Wilma has five IEP goals: two for communication, and three for independent functioning. Her communication goals are:

- To respond positively to an adult interaction by smiling or shaking her head with modeling.
- To match the letters in her first name with physical prompts.

Her independent functioning goals are:

- To identify pictures/symbols paired with words in stories and daily activities accurately and consistently when given one physical prompt and/or hand-over-hand.

- To recognize her name when it is presented with two other names with physical prompts.
- To count play money up to $3, with hand-over-hand.

Joe is an emerging communicator and does so with pointing or gestures. He is ambulatory and is able to feed himself. His primary exceptionality need is Intellectual Disability (InD). He receives occupational therapy and physical therapy services, and has a daily Nursing Care Plan. His priority educational needs are to recognize his name when paired with one other and to follow instruction when given. Some of Joe's strengths include friendliness and smiling with his peers.

Joe has five IEP goals: four for independent functioning, and one for communication.

His independent functioning goals are:

- To sort 10 items by colors with physical assistance.
- To put on his socks and shoes with hand-over-hand assistance.
- To recognize his name when paired with one other name by pointing, given verbal prompts.
- To identify persons, objects and activities by name or characteristics using pictures with modeling when given three verbal prompts.

His communication goal is:

- To express his wants and needs using pictures with modeling when given three verbal or physical prompts.

Kenya communicates verbally. However, there are times when she mumbles her words. Her primary exceptionality is Intellectual Disability (InD). She receives occupational therapy once a month, and has a daily Nursing Care Plan. Her priority educational needs are to make academic choices and participate in school activities more. She loves to help other students in the classroom, give direction and socialize with everyone she knows as she moves about the school.

Kenya has five IEP goals: three for communication, and two for independent functioning. Her communication goals are:

- To indicate verbally or by picture that she needs to use the bathroom with verbal prompts.
- To respond accurately and consistently to pictures/symbols of people, objects or events in familiar stories and daily activities by pointing or speaking with verbal prompts.
- To select preferred or necessary items given two or more options in different activities, in multiple settings with pointing or speaking with verbal prompts.

Her independent functioning goals are:

- To recognize the letters in her name with verbal or physical prompts.
- To sort four sets of items by modeling and verbal prompts.

## Overview of Lesson

The lesson is an ELA lesson with the goal of identifying literary devices. This lesson was on rhyme. The lesson began with a whole group reading of the Dr. Seuss book, *Green Eggs and Ham*. Mr. D. read the book, pausing to ask "Wh" questions here and there. The students had an opportunity to practice identifying rhyming words before breaking off into small groups for deeper discussion and additional reinforcement. Finally, the class came back together as a whole group to participate in an exciting game of *Green Eggs and Ham* Tic Tac Toe.

## Planning

### Long-term Planning

Table 7.1, Long-term Planning, shows how the lesson fits into the yearly planning, which is designed to cover six of the eight units before state testing in late March. After that, the last two units are presented for the rest of the year. This lesson falls within Unit 4, and the lesson meets the following State ELA Access Points:

- LAFS.910.RI.1.AP.3b—Identify connections between key points.
- LAFS.1112.RI.1.AP.3b—Analyze a complex set of ideas or sequence of events and explain how specific individuals, ideas or events interact and develop over the course of the text.

*Table 7.1* Long-term Planning

| Weeks | ELA |
| --- | --- |
| 1–4 | Unit 1—Vocabulary/Fluency |
| 5–7 | Unit 2—Speaking and Listening |
| 8–13 | Unit 3—Comprehension |
| 14–17 | Unit 4—Fiction and Nonfiction |
| 18–22 | Unit 5—Writing Process |
| 23–27 | Unit 6—Types of Writing |
| 28–32 | Unit 7—Real World ELA |
| 33–36 | Unit 8—Technology in ELA |

## *Medium-term Planning*

The medium-term planning is demonstrated in Table 7.2, Medium-term Planning. This lesson is in Unit 4 of the planning.

*Table 7.2* Medium-term Planning

| November 30–January 4 | Unit 4 Fiction/Nonfiction | November Assignments |
|---|---|---|
| | **OVERVIEW**: Students will explore the differences between fiction and nonfiction. They will compare and contrast different genres and their literary devices. | **Weekly Assignment 1:** After reading a fiction text, create a circle map to define the text type using text characteristics. |
| | **Essential Understanding: (Concrete)** Students will build grade-appropriate vocabulary using strategies including context clues and study of word parts. Students will compare and contrast fiction and nonfiction. Students will create a graphic organizer sequencing events of a story correctly. Students will identify symbols of poetry. Students will identify a literacy device. Students will make their own selection of a text. | **Weekly Assignment 2:** After reading a nonfiction text, create a map to define the text type using text. **Weekly Assignment 3:** Use a graphic organizer to compare and contrast the text structures of fiction and nonfiction texts. **Weekly Assignment 4:** After reading a text, complete a graphic organizer constructing the sequence of events. |
| | **Essential Understanding: (Representation)** Students will distinguish the difference between historical fiction and nonfiction. Students will analyze how authors use literacy devices, sentence structure and word choice to manipulate the mood, meaning and purpose of the text. | |
| | **Essential Questions:** How are fiction and nonfiction similar? How are fiction and nonfiction different? Why is it important to know about symbols when reading poetry? What is an example of a literary device? Why is it important to sequence events of a story correctly? | |

### Short-term Planning

Table 7.3 demonstrates the short-term planning that relates to the lesson. The day of this particular lesson is Monday.

*Table 7.3* Short-term Planning

| | Monday | Tuesday | Wednesday | Thursday | Friday |
|---|---|---|---|---|---|
| ELA Skills Review (Includes IEP ELA goals; small group or independent work) | Morning Meeting—Whole Group<br><br>Month, Day, Year: Kenya, Joe<br><br>Weather/Season: Wilma<br><br>Months of the Year: Suzanne | | | | |
| Focus ELA Lesson | Whole group—rhyme words.<br><br>Quick preview of literary devices on Mimio.<br><br>Introduction to vocabulary words: rhyme, rhythm.<br><br>Review of words that rhyme in small group. | Read story as whole group.<br><br>Review vocabulary words.<br><br>Teacher models how to sequence a story (beginning, middle, end).<br><br>Small group and individual practice of skill. | Read story as whole group.<br><br>Review vocabulary words.<br><br>Student practice of the skill of sequencing on the whiteboard during whole group, with support from the teacher, and encouragement from their classmates.<br><br>Small group and individual practice of skill. | Read story as whole group.<br><br>Review vocabulary words.<br><br>Students complete a graphic organizer.<br><br>Class divided to play a team game answering "wh" questions.<br><br>Students color handout. | Final chance to complete weekly assignment and create a graphic organizer showing sequence, with as little support as possible.<br><br>Whole class activity time. |

### Resources Used in the Lesson

- *Mimio*: When using the Mimio, the materials are interactive, meaning they can be manipulated by using a special MimioTeach stylus on the whiteboard.
- *Classroom iPad*: The iPad is used by students who cannot (or, at that moment, prefer not to) use their voice to communicate. The classroom iPad is also used for explicit teaching/demonstration. Mr. D. carries the iPad around the room while teaching to share each screen as an additional visual or to redirect the student, as it may be difficult for the students to keep their focus on the whiteboard for the entire lesson.
- *Boardmaker Studio*: This software is used to create activities that can be used during the instruction of the lesson. This rhyming activity was made interactive so the entire class would be able to participate in the mode of communication they choose: voice, the Mimio or the classroom iPad.
- *TouchChat*: All of the students enjoy using TouchChat, which is customized so that it has the names of everyone in the class, as well as positive and encouraging phrases the students can say to each other. The TouchChats are also continually updated with relevant or lesson-specific vocabulary. For this particular lesson, the words "Green, Eggs, Ham, and Sam-I-Am" were added to the page that contains similar phrases.
- *Printed copies of the handouts*: During the small group portion of the lesson, all students used printed copies of the activity.

## Progress Scale

Scales are used to track student progress for the entire week, not just for one lesson. The learning goal is always Level Three, leaving Level Four to show application of the focus standard for the week. At the beginning of this particular lesson, all four students were ready to begin Level One. Table 7.4 illustrates the Progress Scale used for this lesson.

## The Lesson: Rhyming Literary Device— *Green Eggs and Ham*

The lesson began by reviewing familiar sight words. As the students said the sight word, Mr. D. introduced a word that sounded like the word they just said. They continued to do this for five rounds. During the final round, Mr. D. put the students into smaller groups and challenged them to think of a word that rhymed with the word "hat." All the students were engaged and gave a word they thought rhymed with "hat." One group said "bat," another said "sat" and the third group said "tall." The

*Table 7.4* Progress Scale

| 4 | | I will retell the story using symbols and/or words. |
|---|---|---|
| 3 | | I will complete a graphic organizer showing the sequences of several events. |
| 2 | | I will identify what happens at the beginning of the story. |
| 1 | | I will recognize a character in the story. |

class briefly discussed the answers, and decided to help the third group choose a word that rhymed with "hat." With the assistance of their friends, the third group said "pat." The staff and students gave each other "high-fives" before moving on to the next part in the lesson.

### Whole Group

After the rhyming activity, Mr. D. showed the academic scale and read each level to the students and then asked if they had heard this story before. A couple of them said they had, so Mr. D. asked the students to name a character. Kendra said "Sam." The staff affirmed her and gave her a "high-five." Then, Mr. D. read the story *Green Eggs and Ham*. Level One of the Progress Scale asked the students to name one of the characters in the story. While reading, Mr. D. and the paraprofessionals reminded the students that they were listening for the characters. Mr. D. also defined the protagonist for the students and they also listened for this. After reading the story, Mr. D. read Level Two of the Progress Scale, which asked for what happened at the beginning of the story. This prepared them for the next day's assignment.

*Figure 7.1* Joe achieving Level One of the Progress Scale.

## Small Group

After the skill had been explicitly taught and practiced in the whole group, it was time to break into small groups. As the class divided into their small groups, Mr. D. played some music. Each group had a different activity. One group (Suzanne and Ms. T.) colored a picture of a scene from the story; another group (Wilma, Kenya and Ms. P.) played Tic Tac Toe, while the third group (Joe with Mr. D.) worked on the completion of Level One (naming a character). You can see Joe achieving Level One in Figure 7.1.

The following photographs, Figures 7.2 and 7.3, show Wilma and Suzanne beating Mr. D. in the Tic Tac Toe game.

*Figure 7.2* Wilma beating Mr. D. at Tic Tac Toe.

*Figure 7.3* Suzanne beating Mr. D. at Tic Tac Toe.

During small group time, Mr. D. worked with the students on their mastery of Level One. Ms. E. and Ms. P. worked with the students at the other stations. Figure 7.4 shows Kenya focused on completing the activity independently.

Both Kenya and Wilma finished early and wanted to read the story again. So, while the rest of the class continued their activity, Mr. D. took Kenya and Wilma to a table and re-read part of the story, giving them the opportunity to achieve Level Two. Figure 7.5 shows Kenya identifying her progress (Level Two) on the Progress Scale.

*Figure 7.4* Kenya works independently to color one of the scenes from the story.

*Figure 7.5* Kenya pointing to Level Two of the Progress Scale.

Table 7.5 demonstrates how the personalized targets of the students were naturally integrated into the lesson. This shows that throughout the lesson, Mr. D. was able to meet the personal targets of the students in an enhanced curriculum standards-referenced lesson. It is noted that not all personal student targets were met in this specific lesson.

## Reasons Mr. D. Believes This Was an Effective Lesson (This Section is Written in the First Person)

The school builds specific tasks for every level of the scale, as well as having a learning goal that can be demonstrated by each student. The outcome looks different as each student completes the task. For this particular lesson, Kenya and Wilma reached a Level Two, and Joe and Suzanne mastered Level One. All the students made progress but, being that it was the first day, they did not meet the learning goal yet. I have no doubt that all the students will attain at least the learning goal by the end of the week.

In addition to the learning goal (or, as a support to each student in reaching the learning goal), lessons are designed to feature practice in reading and/or language art skills, such as letters, sight words and spelling (verbally or with the aid of a communication device). Some students may need just a review, and additional practice to reinforce the foundational skills. Students are always encouraged to interact with each other, practicing their social skills by calling each other by name and giving verbal feedback, using their primary mode of communication. I feel that making every lesson as interactive as possible increases the chances the students will comprehend the learning goals in a deeper way.

*Table 7.5* Personal Target Engagement

| Student | Targets | Review |
|---------|---------|--------|
| Suzanne | To be able to sit at her work space (without sweeping items off it). | During the lesson, Suzanne attended to the lesson without swiping the scale or other materials (when placed) off her desk. |
| | To press a switch to initiate an activity upon an adult directive. | Suzanne, in response to a "wh-" question, initiated a switch to demonstrate her answer to the staff. |
| | To place one item in a box with an adult directive and hand-over-hand assistance. | Did not do this during lesson. |
| | To choose between two different foods (when given a choice of two) with verbal prompts. | Did not do this during lesson. |
| Wilma | To respond positively to an adult interaction by smiling or shaking her head with modeling. | Wilma smiled at the staff member when she was asked if she enjoyed listening to the story *Green Eggs and Ham*. |
| | To match the letters in her first name with physical prompts. | When completing the handout, Wilma stamped the letters of her name (on her paper) with hand-over-hand. |
| | To accurately and consistently identify pictures/symbols paired with words in stories and daily activities when given one physical prompt and/or hand-over-hand. | During the reading of *Green Eggs and Ham*, Wilma was able to identify pictures paired with words, accurately. |
| | To recognize her name when it is presented with two other names with physical prompts. | Before beginning the activity, Wilma was asked to find her name from a selection of three choices; she was able to do this after the second chance (with a field of two choices). |
| | To count play money up to $3, with hand-over-hand. | Did not do this during lesson. |

| Joe | To sort 10 items by colors with physical assistance. | Did not do this during lesson. |
|---|---|---|
| | To put on his socks and shoes with hand-over-hand assistance. | Did not do this during lesson. |
| | To recognize his name when paired with one other name by pointing, giving verbal prompts. | Joe was able to recognize his name when given it paired with another student's name, using physical prompts (after first being asked). |
| | To identify persons, objects and activities by name or characteristics using pictures with modeling when given three verbal prompts. | During the reading of Green Eggs and Ham, Joe identified the main character and one activity that happened in the story when verbally asked. |
| | To express his wants and needs using pictures with modeling when given three verbal or physical prompts. | Joe expressed his desire to answer a question, using a picture, when verbally asking the student who would like to go next. |
| Kenya | To indicate verbally or by picture that she needs to use the bathroom with verbal prompts. | Kenya told the staff that she needed to use the restroom, using her words. |
| | To respond accurately and consistently to pictures/symbols of people, objects or events in familiar stories and daily activities by pointing or speaking with verbal prompts. | After reading Green Eggs and Ham, Kenya was able to accurately retell who the main character was and something that happened in the story, when presented with a field of three choices. |
| | To select preferred or necessary items given two or more options in different activities, in multiple settings with pointing or speaking with verbal prompts. | When asked to color her paper, and given a choice of two colors, Kenya said that she would like to use "green" and "blue." |
| | To recognize the letters in her name with verbal or physical prompts. | Before completing her activity page, Kenya stamped her name at the top of the paper, after she picked it out from a selected group of letters. |
| | To sort four sets of items by modeling and verbal prompts. | Did not do this during lesson. |

This lesson was engaging to the students and each student showed success. In addition to creating a positive and enthusiastic environment, I added high interest activities to the lesson (e.g., *Green Eggs and Ham* Tic Tac Toe game, "Name I Am" song and music time). I ensured each student remained on task throughout the lesson, not only during small groups, but in whole group as well. When individual students were demonstrating skills during whole group, the other students were paying attention, because they were expected to give feedback to their friends ("Good job," "Awesome," "Way to go" or "Try again, you can do it," etc.) There is an expectation in the classroom that everyone participates, so it is not unusual for each staff member to provide non-verbal cues or to use proximity to remind the students of their responsibility as a classroom member. During small groups, everyone had their own handout, to keep downtime to a minimum, as well as to keep them from getting distracted. The focus on student engagement shows improvement of their learning, but reduces the potential of behavioral issues.

At Orchard Hills, each student is a unique individual with certain skills and abilities. In order for the teaching staff to meet the needs and wants of the student, they must know each one individually. We pride ourselves on providing lessons in which every student will be able to show success and demonstrate their mastery before moving from one level to the next. This is done in various ways. Technology is a driving force, aiding the students in their primary mode of communication. If any of us observes a student struggling to show mastery of a learning goal using a particular method (direct verbal instruction), we will then present the lesson using a different method (modeling) until the student is able to be successful. Everyone has the ability to communicate, and we feel it is our responsibility to listen to and incorporate the student's mode of communication in everything we present to that particular student.

In this lesson, Direct Instruction was used. It was kept short and direct, to keep the students' attention. However in this lesson, it proved beneficial to use Explicit Instruction, modeling exactly what it looks like when rhyming pairs are needed. I included a lot of repetition and time for practice in this lesson, as I do in each lesson, in each subject area.

The level of support changed as the lesson progressed, using the prompting hierarchy from least to most. This is where the students are not given automatic help for things that they do not need. This goes along with having high expectations for students and appreciating that students are always growing and changing. If the students are not given the opportunity to request what they need they will not be able to show what they can do independently.

Another strategy I used successfully was Flexible Grouping. This involves small groups that change over the course of the day or week. I take into consideration how the students come to school and how they are working up to the point of dividing into smaller groups. I acknowledge the groups in this lesson worked well, with students supporting each other to be successful.

# Chapter 8

# Difficult Decisions?
# Let's Graph it Out!

*With Krysta Avery*

---

This lesson takes place at Orchard Hill School.

## The Classroom

There are seven students in the class, one teacher and two teaching assistants. In addition, support services are received on a weekly basis from an assistive technology teacher, a speech and language pathologist, an occupational therapist and a behavior resource teacher. All students follow state Standard Access Points and have Individualized Education Plans (IEPs). The students are highly interactive and energetic. All of the students have fairly well developed gross motor skills, but most have emerging and developing fine motor skills that are below what is typical for their ages. The grade levels represented by the students are 1st Grade, 3rd Grade, 4th Grade and 5th Grade. One student is a fairly fluent verbal communicator, and two are able to communicate verbally but have very limited vocabulary. Three students have a few words they express verbally, but rely on assistive technology devices for any in-depth or multi-word responses. The final student is developing skills in using an assistive technology device in order to communicate. The classroom follows an Orchard Hill Scope and Sequence curriculum aligned to the state curriculum standards. The materials selected for the academic lessons are standards-based.

## The Adults

Mrs. A. is in her eighth year of teaching. She graduated with a Bachelor of Arts in Psychology with an emphasis in Special Education and a minor in Elementary Education. She began at the school in 2013, after working at a much smaller center school in Michigan. Mrs. A. has always worked primarily with elementary age students, as it is her passion to shape behaviors and teach early learning skills that will positively impact students in the long term in the academic setting. Mrs. K. is one of the paraprofessionals in the class. She has worked at the school for a year and a half, spending almost all of that time in Mrs. A.'s class. She recently moved to Florida, but previously worked as a paraprofessional at a school in New York. Miss J. is the second paraprofessional, who just started working at the school this year. She graduated from college with a Bachelor of Science in Exercise Science. She is also a nanny for two school-aged children.

## The Students

Thomas has early verbal language abilities. His speech skills are emerging, so he uses GoTalk and other teacher created communication boards and communication symbols for communication and vocabulary support. He is ambulatory but does have some delays in his fine motor skills. He is identified under the disability categories of Intellectual Disability (InD) and Speech or Language Impairment (SLI). He receives 30 minutes of small group language therapy each week and 30 minutes of occupational therapy each week. He has daily Special Transportation to and from school, and a daily Nursing Care Plan to monitor his health status because he has Down syndrome.

Thomas has eleven IEP goals: four related to social/emotional behavior, one for independent functioning, two for communication and four related to curriculum.

His social/emotional behavior goals are:

- To comply with one-step directions on first request.
- To follow a morning routine with limited physical assistance.
- To transition through the halls without pushing/touching others.
- To use items without throwing them.

His goal for independent functioning is:

- To pick up and pinch 15 clothes pins with his left hand and clip on a pencil with his right hand.

His communication goals are:

- To use verbs to request and direct others in the classroom, including staff and peers.
- To request needed items.

His curriculum goals are:

- To trace simple lines (straight and diagonal) and trace simple shapes/ forms (cross, circle, square and triangle).
- To match and identify four to five letters in his first name.

- To rote count and count with one-to-one correspondence to six.
- To identify primary colors.

David also has early verbal language abilities. He has echolalia, and also will repeat most things when requested to do so. However, he struggles to produce spontaneous language and recall appropriate vocabulary. He uses GoTalk and other teacher created communication boards and communication symbols for communication and vocabulary support. He is ambulatory and does not have any major health conditions. He is identified under the disability categories of Intellectual Disability (InD) and Speech or Language Impairment (SLI). He receives 30 minutes of small group language therapy each week. A highly structured, individualized Behavior Plan is used with David on a daily basis. He has daily Special Transportation to and from school.

David has two IEP goals: one for communication and one related to curriculum.

His communication goal is:

- To answer wh- (who, what, where) comprehension questions about a story using a two-word response with visual prompts.

His curriculum goal is:

- To correctly add two single-digit numbers using a number line with visual prompts.

Adam has developing language abilities. He is often quiet and takes a fair amount of time to come up with responses. However he very often is able to produce correct one-word responses related to familiar topics and has a rapidly increasing vocabulary. He uses GoTalk and other teacher created communication boards and communication symbols for communication and vocabulary support, but does not rely on them to interact with the curriculum. He was born with spina bifida, but is ambulatory and has fairly well-developed gross and fine motor skills with some minor delays. He does not have any other major health conditions. He is identified under the disability categories of Intellectual Disability (InD) and Speech or Language Impairment (SLI). He receives 60 minutes of small group language therapy each week. A highly structured, individualized Behavior Plan is used with Adam on a daily basis. He has daily Special Transportation to and from school, and a Nursing Care Plan that monitors his health status on a daily basis.

Adam has three IEP goals; two for curriculum and one for communication.

His IEP goals for curriculum are:

- To trace the letters of his name.
- To verbally identify numbers 0–9 when visually shown a number.

His IEP goal for communication is:

- To use three-word combinations including verb + object and adjective + object during structured tasks.

Matthew has fluent verbal language abilities, but needs vocabulary support in areas of academic language. He is a very boisterous student, and often will self-talk during lessons about topics of his own interest. He is quick to supply verbal answers when asked a question. When unsure of an answer or how to respond, he often repeats what was said to him. He uses GoTalk and other teacher created communication boards and communication symbols for vocabulary support only. He is ambulatory and does not have any major health conditions. He has no gross or fine motor delays. He is able to read and write, but does not comprehend most of what he reads. He can copy words and sentences, but is not able to form a complete or grammatically correct sentence when writing. Matthew is identified under the disability categories of Autism Spectrum Disorder (ASD) and Speech or Language Impairment (SLI). He receives 30 minutes of small group language therapy each week. A highly structured, individualized Behavior Plan is used with Matthew on a daily basis. He has daily Special Transportation to and from school.

Matthew has three IEP goals: two for curriculum and one for communication.

His IEP goals for curriculum are:

- To trace the letters of his name.
- To identify numbers 0–9 verbally when visually shown a number.

His IEP goal for communication is:

- To use three-word combinations including verb + object and adjective + object during structured tasks.

Joshua is another student with early verbal language abilities. He is very reluctant to talk, but is slowly developing a larger spoken vocabulary. He struggles a great deal to produce spontaneous language. Even when prompted and given a verbal model, he has a great deal of difficulty repeating or even making a close approximation of the words. He uses GoTalk and other teacher created communication boards and communication symbols for communication and vocabulary support.

He is ambulatory, but has some limitations with fine motor skills. He has a medical diagnosis of Down syndrome. He is identified under the disability categories of Intellectual Disability (InD) and Speech or Language Impairment (SLI). He receives 30 minutes of small group language therapy each week, as well as 30 minutes of occupational therapy on a weekly basis. He also has a Nursing Care Plan to monitor his health. A highly structured, individualized Behavior Plan is used with Joshua on a daily basis. He has daily Special Transportation to and from school.

Joshua has two IEP goals: one for communication and one related to curriculum.

His communication goal is:

• To use two-word combinations, including verb + object and adjective + object with visual supports.

His curriculum goal is:

• To trace the letters of his name independently.

Jason has strong receptive language skills, but has early expressive/verbal language skills. He makes vocalizations to attempt to communicate, but they are mostly unintelligible. He uses TouchChat, GoTalk and other teacher created communication boards and communication symbols for communication and vocabulary support. He is ambulatory and does not have any major health conditions. He is identified under the disability categories of Intellectual Disability (InD) and Speech or Language Impairment (SLI). He receives 60 minutes of small group language therapy each week. A highly structured, individualized Behavior Plan is used with Jason on a daily basis. He has daily Special Transportation to and from school.

Jason has two IEP goals: one for communication and one related to curriculum.

His communication goal is:

• To demonstrate comprehension of and use picture symbols with voice output to describe objects using 10 adjectives related to size, temperature, speed and color.

His curriculum goal is:

• To copy the letters of his name and write them with good form using a visual support.

## Overview of Lesson

The lesson is a Math lesson collecting data from each student about which type of hat they would like everyone to make for the Thanksgiving celebration and organizing that data in a graph to represent the results. Collecting the class votes (data) would facilitate representing the results in a graph, giving a visual representation of the results, as well as the decision of what hat to make.

## Lesson Learning Goal

Students will use data collection to create a graphing model that represents the results of a question.

## Planning

### Long-term Planning

Table 8.1, Long-term Planning, shows how the lesson fits into the yearly planning, which is designed to cover all six units before the state testing in early March. After that, four of the units are reviewed over the rest of the year. This lesson falls within Unit 4. The lesson meets the following State Access Math Points:

- MAFS.1.MD.3.AP.4a—Analyze data by sorting into two categories; answer questions about the total number of data points and how many in each category.
- MAFS.1.MD.3.AP.4b—Using a picture graph, represent each object/person counted on the graph (1:1 correspondence) for two or more categories.
- MAFS.1.MD.3.AP.4c—Compare the values of the two categories of data in terms of more or less.
- MAFS.3.MD.2.AP.3a—Collect data and organize into a picture or bar graph.
- MAFS.5.G.1.AP.1a—Locate the x- and y-axis on a coordinate plane.

### Medium-term Planning

This is demonstrated in Table 8.2, Medium-term Planning. This lesson sits within Unit 4 of the planning.

### Short-term Planning

Table 8.3 demonstrates the short-term planning that relates to the lesson. The day of this particular lesson is Monday.

*Table 8.1* Long-term Planning

| Weeks | Math |
| --- | --- |
| 1–3 | Unit 1—Number Basics |
| 4–6 | Unit 2—Number Computation |
| 7–10 | Unit 3—Fractions |
| 11–15 | Unit 4—Measurement and Graphs |
| 16–20 | Unit 5—Polygons |
| 21–25 | Unit 6—3D Shapes |
| 26–28 | Unit 4—Measurement and Graphs |
| 29–31 | Unit 3—Fractions |
| 32–34 | Unit 2—Number Computation |
| 35–37 | Unit 1—Number Basics |

*Table 8.2* Medium-term Planning

| November 3–December 7 | Unit 4 Measurement and Graphs | November Assignments |
| --- | --- | --- |

November 3–
December 7

*Unit 4*
*Measurement and Graphs*

**OVERVIEW**:

**Essential Understanding:
(Concrete)**
Students will choose an appropriate measuring tool.
Students will estimate the measure of various objects.
Students will use the appropriate measuring tool when solving problems.
Students will identify types of graphs.
Students will identify the separate elements of a graph.

**Essential Understanding:
(Representation)**
Students will compare lengths, heights and weights using words like longer, shorter, heavier, lighter, etc.
Students will order objects by their length.
Students will use measurements to complete formulas to find area, perimeter, etc.

*November Assignments*

**Weekly Assignment 1:**
Match measuring tools to the items they are used with (scale, measuring tape, tablespoon, etc.).

**Weekly Assignment 2:**
Measure an item using at least one conventional and at least one non-conventional measuring tool.

**Weekly Assignment 3:**
With a measuring tool, determine the perimeter of a shape.

**Weekly Assignment 4:**
Select the correct graph that matches a given scenario and/or equation.

**Weekly Assignment 5:**
Use data collection to create a graphing model that represents results of a question.

Students will create a graph to represent a real-world situation.

Students will draw and interpret graphs of relations.

Students will compare mean, median and modes.

Students will collect and organize data.

**Essential Questions:**

How can we use measurement in our daily lives?

How can we tell which of the two objects is longer than the other?

How do we compare, order and measure length, height and weight?

How do we know which tool to use?

Why do we estimate measurement?

When do we estimate measurement?

How can we collect data?

What type of data can you collect?

How do tables help us organize data?

How do we choose the appropriate graph for the situation?

Why is it important to label graphs?

How can graphing data help analyze it?

Why do we use central tendency?

**Mathematical Practices:**

MAFS.K12.MP.5.1—Use appropriate tools strategically.

*Choose appropriate tools for your problem.

*Use mathematical tools correctly and efficiently.

*Estimate and use what you know to check the answers you find using tools.

MAFS.K.12.MP.6.1—Attend to precision.

*Communicate your mathematical thinking clearly and precisely.

*Use the level of precision you need for your problem.

*Be accurate when you count.

*Table 8.3* Short-term Planning

|         | Monday | Tuesday | Wednesday | Thursday | Friday |
|---------|--------|---------|-----------|----------|--------|
| Focus Math Lesson | Warm up activity identifying graphs in pictures on the Mimio. | Warm up activity identifying graphs in pictures on the Mimio. | Warm up activity identifying graphs in pictures on the Mimio. | Warm up activity identifying graphs in pictures on the Mimio. | Warm up activity identifying graphs in pictures on the Mimio. |
|         | Presentation of question – What type of Thanksgiving hat would you like to make? | Review of poll result on Mimio presentation (whole group). | Review poll results on table on Mimio presentation (whole group). | Review poll results on table on Mimio presentation (whole group). | Review poll results on table on Mimio presentation (whole group). |
|         | Participating in a poll on the Mimio presentation. | Representing poll results in a table (small group). | Create a pictograph of results (small group). | Create a bar graph of results (small group). | Create a bar graph on Boardmaker software (individual). |
|         |        |         |           | Interpret the data results using Mimio presentation (whole group). | Create the winning hat choice (whole group). |

## Resources Used in the Lesson

- *Mimio*: When using the Mimio, the materials are interactive, meaning they can be manipulated by using either a special Mimio pen on the whiteboard or by using a classroom iPad, which has the whiteboard porting to it. The Mimio presentation used was created and customized by the teacher specifically for this lesson.
- *Student iPads with GoTalk Communication Software*: Each student has an iPad that they use for communication and interaction with classroom activities. There are communication boards that are created by the teacher and loaded on to the iPad before the lesson. Each student has communication boards that are customized for his or her individual needs. These communication boards include vocabulary words chosen by the teacher or speech-language pathologist and can have varying numbers of symbols/vocabulary words per page. The communication software has voice output so the students can respond

and "verbally" participate in class activities even with limited verbal language skills.

- *Printed pictograph worksheet*: Each student was provided with an individual worksheet that had the x and y axes printed and labeled, and with symbols for the pictograph already cut out so they only had to be pasted on to the appropriate area of the graph. The graphs were designed with a one-to-one correspondence, so each symbol was representative of one vote.
- *Boardmaker Studio*: Each student had the availability of a graphing extension activity through the Boardmaker studio software. Students were able to use a graphing activity created by Mrs. A. on Boardmaker studio software to create a graph of the results of the graphing question on the iPad. This was an additional activity to the printed activity on paper for all students. This was an extra extension activity for students who quickly finished the printed worksheet.

## Progress Scale

Scales are used to track student progress for the entire week, not just for one lesson. The learning goal is always Level Three, so that there is always room for a Level Four assignment that makes sure even the higher level students are challenged. This lesson was new to the students, so all of the students started on Level One. Students will sometimes progress through more than one level in a day, and other days spend most of the time working on one particular level. Student needs and ability levels determine the amount of time spent on each level. This lesson provides the opportunity for a student to progress through all four levels in one day, if able. For this lesson, students had just started working on creating graphs. The lesson was repeated each day after this initial teaching to see that students were able to consistently perform and retain the skills related to it. Table 8.4 illustrates the Progress Scale used for this lesson.

## The Lesson: Difficult Decisions? Let's Graph it Out!

The lesson began with presenting a question to the class. Students were asked what type of hat they would like to make for the upcoming Thanksgiving celebration. In the previous week, students had begun learning about the voting process as part of the Social Studies unit. Students were guided to the idea that they would be able to vote on which hat they would like, but since everyone is going to make the same type of hat, a decision must be made. Students had pictures of each type of hat, a turkey hat or a pilgrim hat, to use as symbols representing a vote. Students cast votes on a ballot, then used a t-chart as a whole class to separate the

*Table 8.4* Progress Scale

| 4 | Which had more?   Which had less? | **I will interpret the data collected.** |
|---|---|---|
| 3 | Which Thanksgiving hat should the class make?<br> | **I will use data collection to create a graphing model that represents results of a question.** |
| 2 | | **I will sort the data collected.** |
| 1 | Which Thanksgiving hat should the class make?<br> | **I will participate in a poll.** |

votes. The total was counted for each type of hat. Finally, the number of turkey hats and the number of pilgrim hats were represented on a pictograph that each student made individually. Students were able to practice all of these steps as a whole group, and were then given practice opportunities to make their own graph individually.

## *Whole Group, Small Group and Individual Work*

As a whole group, the students were reminded that they were learning about graphs this week, and were given a bell-ringer activity to get them engaged in the concept of graphs. Students were shown a group of pictures that had graphs within them, like a newspaper article or page of a book. They were then able to each take a turn to come to the front of the classroom and use the interactive whiteboard to locate the graph. All of the students found a graph independently, or with some guidance from a teacher showing them the text on the page and the graph with the prompt, "Which one is the graph?" Thomas and David needed the questioning support, while the rest of the students were able to locate a graph on their own. Students were then connected to the idea of making their own graph by Mrs. A. presenting a problem. She told the students she would like to make a Thanksgiving hat with them for the upcoming holiday, but she didn't know if they should choose a pilgrim hat or a turkey hat. This group of students enjoys making and wearing hats, so they were quickly interested and engaged in this problem. Mrs. A. reminded them that since they had learned about voting in Social Studies, they could take a vote and graph the results to find out who was the winner. The Mimio presentation was used with pictures of the students and pictures of each type of hat. Each student got the opportunity to cast a vote for a pilgrim hat or a turkey hat. Then, the next slide had a table that allowed the votes to be sorted. Figure 8.1 shows David casting his vote.

*Figure 8.1* David casting his vote.

Mrs. A. modeled for the students how to sort the items on the chart. Then, students worked in groups of two with an adult support to complete a sort on their own. Matthew, Adam, Jason, David and Joshua needed very little teacher support to complete this task. Thomas needed prompting, with Mrs. K. asking him for each vote "What did they vote for?" and "Where does it go?"

Students returned to whole group instruction to count up the results on the table. After each side was counted, Mrs. A. told them they were ready to make a graph. On the Mimio presentation, students were shown how to create a pictograph and a bar graph by Mrs. A. Then, the students returned to the small group setting to each make an individual graph. All of the students chose to make a pictograph, and were given a graph outline and small pictures of turkey hats and pilgrim hats. They were guided by Mrs. A., Mrs. K. and Miss J. to count out the correct number for each side and glue them on the graph. Joshua and Thomas needed help with applying glue, but were able to count along with teacher prompting to find the correct number of each hat. Matthew and David were able to create a graph on their own with very little teacher guidance, other than encouragement that they were on the right track and doing a great job. Adam and Jason needed support counting the correct amounts, but were able to glue them in the correct place on the graph with minimal teacher assistance, other than occasional pointing to remind them where to glue and keep them on task. Figure 8.2 shows Thomas wearing the hat that won the vote.

*Figure 8.2* Thomas wearing the hat that won the vote.

*Table 8.5* Personal Target Engagement

| Student | Targets | Review |
|---------|---------|--------|
| Thomas | To comply with one-step directions on first request. | Thomas was able to work on this target in the lesson by following directions related to completing his graph. |
| | To use items without throwing them. | Thomas used the iPad and worksheet for graphing. He successfully used these items without throwing them for the duration of the lesson. |
| | To use verbs to request and direct others in the classroom, including staff and peers. | This was not a main focus during this specific lesson. |
| | To request needed items. | Thomas needed glue to complete his graph. He had to be prompted to ask for glue ("What do you need?" "Ask for the glue.") He was able to say, "Glue, please," when given a model. |
| | To rote count and count with one-to-one correspondence to six. | While organizing the votes for each type of hat, Thomas was able to practice counting to find the total. He needed a fair amount of prompting to touch each vote and say the number. |
| David | To answer wh- (who, what, where) comprehension questions about a story using a two-word response with visual prompts. | This target of David's was not specifically incorporated into this lesson. |
| | To correctly add two single-digit numbers using a number line with visual prompts. | This target of David's was not specifically incorporated into this lesson. |
| Adam | To verbally identify the numbers 0–9 when visually shown a number. | This target was met when creating the graph. Adam had to identify the correct number on the "y" axis of the graph to correctly graph the total number of votes. He was successful. |
| | To use three-word combinations including verb + object and adjective + object during structured tasks. | Adam used three-word combinations verbally and with his device to respond to teacher questions during the lesson. He only needed limited modeling or prompting. |

*Table 8.5* Continued

| Student | Targets | Review |
| --- | --- | --- |
| Matthew | To trace the letters of his name. | Matthew did not engage with target during the lesson. |
| | To verbally identify the numbers 0–9 when visually shown a number. | This target was met when creating the graph. Matthew had to identify the correct number on the "y" axis of the graph to correctly graph the total number of votes. He was successful. |
| | To use three-word combinations including verb + object and adjective + object during structured tasks. | Matthew used three-word combinations verbally and with his device to respond to teacher questions during the lesson. He only needed limited modeling or prompting. |
| Joshua | To use two-word combinations, including verb + object and adjective + object with visual supports. | Joshua used two-word combinations during the lesson with his device to respond to a teacher's question. |
| Jason | To demonstrate comprehension of and use picture symbols with voice-output to describe objects using 10 adjectives related to size, temperature, speed and color. | Jason responded to teacher questions using his communication device. However, adjectives were not extensively worked on or related to this lesson. He was able to say which hat had more votes and which had less, and answer teacher questions throughout the lesson. |

Table 8.5 demonstrates how the personalized targets of the students were naturally integrated into the lesson. This shows that throughout the lesson, Mrs. A. was able to meet the personal targets of all the students except David. However, David achieved Level 3 of the lesson progress scale.

## Reflection on the Strategies Used in the Lesson

Errorless learning is always used in the lessons in Mrs. A's classroom. Guiding the students to the correct answer helps them build success rather than feel frustrated by not answering questions correctly. Each student may need a different level of support to achieve the same task. However, all students are expected to, and given the chance to, participate to the fullest extent possible. Many of these modifications have to be done quickly in that moment, and it takes quick thinking and constant informal assessment of student needs and performance to make adjustments. For example, a student can be asked a question in a traditional, more open-ended manner, but may not know how to respond. This question might be "What type of hat would you like to make?" If a student is unable to answer, it can be narrowed down to "Would you like to make a turkey hat or pilgrim hat?" If the student is still unsure how to answer, we can use physical prompting and/or pointing to show them where the symbols are on the communication board to guide them to a response. This support, starting at least restrictive and increasing as it goes on, is an important strategy to see a student's independent abilities while still guiding them to participate in the lesson.

The students had a high level of engagement during this lesson because it tapped into an ongoing interest many of the students in the classroom had, which was creating hats that they could wear around the school that are related to different things going on in the school or curriculum. The students had shown a great deal of interest in Dr. Seuss hats, as well as other holiday hats earlier in the school year, so a high amount of interest in discussing which hat to make made the students very excited to participate in the lesson. All of the students in this class enjoy going up to the front of the classroom to use the Mimio board. They like having the opportunity to get out of their seats, as well as the praise and attention with completing the task in front of their peers. They are also very highly motivated by using technology when completing academic tasks, such as the iPad and communication software. The subject matter and mode of completing the tasks related to the lesson motivate the students a great deal and create a high amount of student engagement. Having their own iPad to work with, as well as individual worksheets, provided students with a maximum amount of time to be engaged in work tasks and very little downtime when they were required to sit and wait. Additionally, even when whole group instruction is being used, Mrs. K. and Miss J. sit near the students and ask questions or redirect to keep them interested. This essentially provides small group instruction within the whole group instruction setting to keep students engaged and attending to the lesson and the task at hand.

Besides the obvious skills being taught in this lesson related to Math and graphing, there are two overarching things that Mrs. A. always includes as an integral part of her lessons and her classroom environment: behavior and communication instruction. All of the students in Mrs. A.'s class have usually started with a significant lack of knowledge and experience with the learning and social behaviors that are necessary to be successful in a school setting and in the classroom environment. Knowing how to be ready to learn: sitting in your seat, having nice learning hands and using an inside voice. Working together and sharing are always emphasized at the beginning of lessons and many times throughout. The students are always given lots of positive reinforcement for following the classroom rules and have even begun to remind each other to follow the rules, either verbally or using a communication device. The students need a predictable environment with a predictable progression through the lessons to be able to participate successfully. A combination of having clear behavior expectations and clear learning goals, which are both explicitly taught using the learning scale, allows the students to be able to access the lessons and learn more easily in the classroom.

Communication is also something that has to be explicitly taught. Students are learning the vocabulary words available on the iPad communication software, but are also learning when to press the buttons and give a response. They are constantly receiving additional instruction as needed from Mrs. A., Mrs. K. and Miss J. about how to give an appropriate response (only pressing the buttons one time, using the appropriate vocabulary, waiting for their turn to speak, etc.). Integrating appropriate communication and appropriate behavior into the academic lessons maximizes student learning and provides the greatest opportunity for maximized student engagement.

## Reasons Mrs. A. Believes This Was an Effective Lesson (This Section is Written in the First Person)

The students were very excited to complete this lesson because it was relevant to them in the sense that they were choosing which hat they could make. They were so motivated about the hats and the upcoming holiday, they did not see this task as work at all. I had real examples of the hats to show them, which they found very exciting to look at. The students also love the opportunity to get out of their seats and come to the front of the class to make a choice, so they were very enthusiastic for the opportunity to interact with the content on the Mimio presentation. Even when students did not know the answer or were unsure what to do, errorless learning strategies were presented so that the students would have success and get the correct answer. All students were able to participate in the lesson, regardless of skill level or background knowledge at the beginning of the lesson. I teach graphing more than once throughout the school year, with repeat opportunities for students to build on their skills.

# Chapter 9

# Perfect Pairs— Finding Animals on the Coordinate Plane

*With Kristen Kasha*

---

This lesson takes place at Orchard Hill School.

## The Classroom Community

It is worth taking some time to learn about how the teacher, Ms. K., approaches the facilitation of her learning community in the classroom. She carefully sets up the classroom to support the students' engagement and interaction with the world outside of themselves. Communication is a priority and group communication is taught explicitly. Ms. K. believes communication goes beyond communicating the answer to a curriculum-based lesson and that social communication, interaction with peers and friends, is healthy and desirable. All students in the class have their own devices with voice output and Ms. K. has structured the learning community to offer opportunities for students to connect with their peers. She has built time into group work for all students to connect by using symbols in order to communicate each other's names and to comment on their friends' responses to the lesson. They each have symbols to communicate "Good job," "Try again," "You go, girl," "You can do it!" This has become a very successful way to build up the students' understanding that through their AAC device their voice can be heard through experiencing the joy of speaking and being heard. Their social vocabulary grows as they learn new things to tell each other. Their academic vocabulary grows as they stay more attentive to lessons and how their peers are responding.

## The Classroom

There are six students in the class, along with one teacher and two paraprofessionals. One of the students, Carla, also has a full-time nurse who comes to class with her. All of the students are on the state Standard Access Points, and all of them have Individualized Education Plans (IEPs). Most of the students have mobility and fine motor issues. Three students are non-verbal, and three have limited verbal skills. All six students have

Alternative Augmentative Communication (AAC) devices. The students are taught in whole group, small group and individualized settings, with an emphasis on the use of technology. The classroom follows an Orchard Hill created Scope and Sequence that is modified from the one the district uses, and aligned to the state standards Access Points. The materials selected or created for the academic lessons are based on these Access Points, and not on a specific curriculum.

## The Adults

Ms. K. is in her tenth year of teaching. She graduated with a Bachelor of Arts in Psychology and Religion in 2004. She entered the teaching profession in 2006 and pursued a teaching certification in elementary education before pursuing a Master of Education in Exceptional Student Education. As part of this program she received her State Autism Spectrum Disorder (ASD) endorsement. She began at the school in 2013 and has spent her time in the middle and high school classes. She serves on the school curriculum writing team. Mrs. M. is a paraprofessional in the class and is currently pursuing her Bachelor of Arts in Liberal Arts. She has been at this school for 4 years and in this classroom for 2 years. Mrs. M. has previously managed a daycare she owned. Miss. S. is a paraprofessional and is currently working towards a degree in Interdisciplinary Studies. She has been at the school for 3 years and in this classroom for 1 year. She had worked in a residential group home for 7 months before coming to the school. Miss. S. has a younger brother with ASD. Nurse C. has been a Licensed Practice Nurse (LPN) since 1976, and she has been with Carla since 2007. This is the second year she and Carla have been in the class.

## The Students

Isadora uses TouchChat on the iPad as her AAC. She uses a wheelchair, and is fed through a G-tube. Her primary exceptionalities are Orthopedic Impairment (OI) and Speech or Language Impairment (SLI), for which she receives 30 minutes' small group language therapy each week. For Related Services, she receives occupational therapy for 30 minutes twice a month, and monitoring for physical therapy once every 9 weeks. She also has daily Special Transportation and a daily Nursing Care Plan. Her priority educational need is to navigate her assistive technology devices more independently. Her strengths are that she is highly motivated to use her AAC, and that she has made a lot of progress with this already. She likes to work as independently on it as possible. She is also very social: she loves to visit with people, and communicate with her classmates.

Isadora has four IEP goals: three for communication and one for independent functioning. Her communication goals are:

- To use picture symbols representing language concepts to describe photographs.
- To use picture symbols representing specific action words.
- To use picture symbols to request the items needed to complete a vocational task.

Her independent functioning goal is:

- To press a switch within 5 seconds after receiving an indirect cue.

Carla also uses TouchChat on the iPad as her AAC. She also uses a wheelchair and is fed through a G-tube. She has a full-time private nurse come to school with her, due to her fragile medical condition and risk of seizures. Her primary exceptionalities are Other Health Impairment (OHI) and Speech or Language Impairment (SLI), for which she receives 30 minutes of small group language therapy each week. For Related Services, she receives occupational therapy for 30 minutes each week, and monitoring for physical therapy once every 9 weeks. She also has daily Special Transportation and a daily Nursing Care Plan. When answering questions, Carla often takes extra time and/or "hovers" over an answer without officially choosing it, often waiting for adult prompting or feedback. She also has a high number of absences, which affects her rate of learning. Her priority educational need is to increase the vocabulary she is comfortable communicating with. One of her strengths is Math— she has good number recognition and early counting skills.
   Carla has four IEP goals: three for communication and one for independent functioning. Her communication goals are:

- To use a dynamic display device to answer an academic question within 10 seconds.
- To use a dynamic display device to locate and select specific nouns.
- To use picture symbols to request the items needed to complete a vocational task.

Her independent functioning goal is:

- To press a switch for at least 90 seconds.

Joy has some early verbal skills with imprecise articulation that make her almost unintelligible for someone who is not a familiar listener. She uses a Dynavox with dual switch scanning as her AAC. She uses a wheelchair and has limited vision. Her primary exceptionalities are Orthopedic Impairment (OI), Visual Impairment (VI), for which she receives 60 minutes of individualized instruction each week, and Speech or Language Impairment

(SLI). She receives 45 minutes of small group and 15 minutes of individualized instruction each week for the language impairment, as well as 15 minutes of small group and 15 minutes of individualized instruction each week for the speech impairment. For Related Services, she receives occupational therapy for 30 minutes each week, and physical therapy for 30 minutes each week. She also has daily Special Transportation, a daily Nursing Care Plan and a daily Behavior Intervention Plan (BIP). Her priority educational needs are to communicate her wants and needs (both verbally and through the use of assistive technology) and to demonstrate her comprehension of academic subjects independently through the use of technology. Joy uses dual switch scanning to complete most of her academic work in the classroom. Most of this work is in the form of scanning-enabled Boardmaker programs that are created for the whole class, specially designed to cover the main idea of every subject, and to be completed as independently as possible. She also uses dual switch scanning with a Dynavox to do a lot of her communication. Some of her strengths include great memorization and spelling skills. She is currently working on spelling out words in order to aid in understanding her words that are unintelligible.

Joy has ten IEP goals: six for curriculum and learning, two for independent functioning and two for communication. Her curriculum and learning goals are:

- To use a customized computer to complete an activity involving matching, categorizing, labeling or sequencing.
- To spell at least five words from a personal familiar word list correctly each day.
- To use a customized computer to create an accurate sentence using a word bank and including proper punctuation.
- To ask or answer academic questions on her Dynavox.
- To locate five images from the CVI Complexity Sequences kit.
- To identify at least five letters in upper or lowercase form each day, with mastery of 15 letters in both forms as a final goal.

Her independent functioning goals are:

- To independently advance her gait trainer 125 feet.
- To grasp and pull down a reciprocal pulley with a weight of 4 pounds.

Her communication goals are:

- To use a variety of preprogrammed phrases on her Dynavox to interact with and direct others to complete routine-based classroom activities.
- To repeat a list or phrase of up to three words maintaining syllable boundaries.

Steve has some early verbal skills with imprecise articulation. He sometimes repeats words or sings along to parts of songs, but the majority of the time he chooses not to communicate verbally. He uses TouchChat on the iPad as his AAC. He has a diagnosis of Down syndrome. His primary exceptionalities include Intellectual Disability (InD) and Speech or Language Impairment (SLI), for which he receives 30 minutes of small group language therapy each week. For Related Services, he has daily Special Transportation and a daily Nursing Care Plan. His priority educational needs are to be able to communicate as effectively as possible and to be able to work independently on tasks. His strengths include using his AAC device, on which he has made amazing progress this past year. He is using it to initiate and maintain interactions with his teachers and his peers. He also loves to help other students in the classroom.

Steve has four IEP goals: one for communication, two for independent functioning and one for curriculum and learning. His communication goal is:

- To use a dynamic display device to locate specific adjectives and verbs.

His independent functioning goals are:

- To fill out his basic personal information onto a modified application form from a model.
- To sort and fold laundry of at least four different types.

His curriculum and learning goal is:

- To identify coins.

Bruce also has early verbal skills and uses one- to three-word phrases to communicate his needs or respond to academic questions. He can imitate with a verbal model and is beginning to use TouchChat on the iPad as AAC. His primary exceptionalities include Intellectual Disability (InD) and Speech or Language Impairment (SLI), for which he receives 30 minutes of small group language therapy each week. For Related Services, he has daily Special Transportation and a daily Nursing Care Plan. His priority educational needs are to increase his functional communication and expressive language skills. His strengths include showing good effort on academic tasks and a willingness to try new things.

Bruce has four IEP goals: two for communication and two for independent functioning. His communication goals are:

- To use a dynamic display device to locate and select specific nouns.
- To use picture symbols to request the items needed to complete a prevocational task.

His independent functioning goals are:

- To sort and fold laundry.
- To work on a prevocational task for at least 10 minutes.

Tony uses TouchChat on the iPad as his AAC. He has some marked difficulty walking and maneuvering around the classroom. His primary exceptionalities include Other Health Impairment (OHI) and Speech or Language Impairment (SLI), for which he receives 60 minutes of small group language therapy each week. For Related Services, he receives monitoring for occupational therapy once every 9 weeks and daily Special Transportation. His priority educational needs are to increase his communicative output and to communicate multiple thoughts on a topic. His strengths include great usage of his AAC device, where he often communicates spontaneous thoughts.

Tony has four IEP goals: two for communication, one for independent functioning and one for curriculum and learning. His communication goals are:

- To answer questions on his AAC using past, future and/or present progressive verb tenses.
- To use his AAC device to create multiple sentences on a given topic.

His independent functioning goal is:

- to identify time by 15-minute intervals on an analog clock.

His curriculum and learning goal is:

- To add and subtract sums to 100 with the use of a large button calculator.

## Overview of Lesson

The lesson is a Math lesson on plotting ordered pairs. It began with a whole group review of counting super heroes. This progressed to counting along a number line together. Symbols of animals were used to model how to count and plot an ordered pair on a coordinate plane. The students practiced as a whole group before moving to individual practice with their own grids.

## Lesson Learning Goal

Students will plot at least one ordered pair on a coordinate plane.

# Planning

## Long-term Planning

Table 9.1, Long-term Planning, shows how the lesson fits into the yearly planning, which is designed to cover all six units before the state testing in early March. After that, four of the units are reviewed over the rest of the year. This lesson falls within Unit 3. It meets the following state Math Access Points:

- MAFS.6.NS.3.AP.8a—Graph or identify points in all four quadrants of the coordinate plane, given a coordinate plane on graph paper.
- MAFS.7.RP.1.AP.2a—Identify the rate of change/proportional relationship of a linear equation that has been plotted as a line on a coordinate plane.
- MAFS.8.EE.3.AP.8a—Identify the coordinates of the point of intersection for two linear equations plotted on a coordinate plane.

## Medium-term Planning

This is demonstrated in Table 9.2, Medium-term Planning. This lesson sits within Unit 3 of the planning.

## Short-term Planning

Table 9.3 demonstrates the short-term planning that relates to the lesson. The day of this particular lesson is Wednesday.

*Table 9.1* Long-term Planning

| Weeks | Math |
| --- | --- |
| 1–3 | Unit 1—Number Basics |
| 4–6 | Unit 2—Equations |
| 7–10 | Unit 3—Points and Lines |
| 11–15 | Unit 4—Measurement and Graphs |
| 16–20 | Unit 5—Polygons |
| 21–25 | Unit 6—3D Shapes |
| 26–28 | Unit 4—Measurement and Graphs |
| 29–31 | Unit 3—Points and Lines |
| 32–34 | Unit 2—Equations |
| 35–37 | Unit 1—Number Basics |

*Table 9.2* Medium-term Planning

| October 5– October 27 | Unit 3 Points and Lines | October Assignments |
|---|---|---|

**October 5– October 27** *Unit 3 Points and Lines*

*October Assignments*

**OVERVIEW**: Students will review different types of lines, ordered pairs and how they relate to coordinate grids and data tables.

**Essential Understanding: (Concrete)**
Students will identify a line segment.
Students will identify parallel and perpendicular lines.
Students will locate points using ordered pairs of numbers.
Students will identify points on a coordinate system (i.e., a simple map represented on a grid).
Students will locate points using ordered pairs.

**Essential Understanding: (Representation)**
Students will compare parallel lines and perpendicular lines.
Students will distinguish between a point, a line and a line segment.
Students will organize data onto a line plot.
Students will complete transformations on grids.

**Essential Questions:**
How do you differentiate between the midpoint and ends of a line segment?
How can you differentiate between parallel lines and perpendicular lines?
How do you determine the location of a point in a coordinate system?
How is a coordinate plane system used in everyday life?

**Mathematical Practices:**

**MAFS.K12.MP.3.1**—Construct viable arguments and critique the reasoning of others.
*Explain both what to do and why it works.
*Work to make sense of others' mathematical thinking.

**Weekly Assignment 1:**
Identify the angles on a polygon.

**Weekly Assignment 2:**
Construct a line parallel to a given line through a point not on the line.

**Weekly Assignment 3:**
Construct perpendicular lines from a given line.

**Weekly Assignment 4:**
Plot coordinate pairs on a grid.

*Table 9.3* Short-term Planning

| | Monday | Tuesday | Wednesday | Thursday | Friday |
|---|---|---|---|---|---|
| *Math Skills Review*<br><br>*(Includes IEP Math goals; small group or independent work)* | Calendar Math—Whole Group<br><br>Telling Time: Bruce, Tony<br><br>Shape Recognition and Matching: Joy, Carla, Isadora<br><br>Counting and Addition Skills: Bruce, Isadora, Joy<br><br>Practicing with a Calculator: Tony, Steven<br><br>Identifying Money: Steven, Carla | | | | |
| Focus Math Lesson | Small group practice counting manipulatives with one-to-one correspondence.<br><br>Quick preview of coordinate pairs on Mimio.<br><br>Introduction to vocabulary words: across, up.<br><br>Review of number lines on Mimio during whole group. | Full introduction to coordinate pairs on Mimio.<br><br>Review vocabulary words.<br><br>Teacher demonstration on how to plot coordinate pairs on a grid.<br><br>Small group and individual practice of skill. | Review coordinate pairs on Mimio.<br><br>Review vocabulary words.<br><br>Student practice of the skill on the whiteboard during whole group, with support from the teacher, and encouragement from their classmates.<br><br>Small group and individual practice of skill. | Review coordinate pairs on Mimio.<br><br>Review vocabulary words.<br><br>More supported student demonstrations on whiteboard.<br><br>Additional opportunities for small group and individual practice of skill. | Final chance to complete weekly assignment and plot coordinate pairs on a grid with as little support as possible.<br><br>Documentation of student work for records. |

## Resources Used in the Lesson

- *Mimio*: When using the Mimio, the materials are interactive, meaning they can be manipulated by using either a special MimioTeach Stylus on the whiteboard, or by using a classroom iPad, which has the whiteboard porting to it.

- *Classroom iPad*: Everything done on the iPad has a real time effect on what is happening on the screen, so the whole class can see the work that an individual student is doing. The iPad is employed for students who cannot (or, at that moment, prefer not to) leave their seats to come up to the board. The classroom iPad is also used for explicit teaching/demonstration. Ms. K. carries the iPad around the room while teaching to share the screen as an additional visual aid or attention getter, as it may be difficult for the students to keep their focus on the whiteboard. A magnifying feature of the Mimio on the iPad is used to focus on specific parts of the screen to exemplify a specific skill, for example, counting along a number line.
- *Boardmaker Studio*: This software was used for two purposes. First, to develop a personalized communication board for Isadora. Communication boards made with Boardmaker Online have voice output, so Isadora was able to communicate in a way that everyone, including her peers, can hear. Second, to create a counting activity that was used during the introduction of the lesson. This counting activity was made interactive for the whole class with the use of the Mimio and classroom iPad.
- *TouchChat*: For this lesson, Tony, Carla, Bruce and Steven used TouchChat on their personal iPads. All of them use the 42 Basic Wordpower Vocabulary. All of their TouchChats are customized so that they have the names of everyone in the class, as well as positive and encouraging phrases they can tell each other. The TouchChats are also continually updated with relevant or lesson-specific vocabulary. For this particular lesson, the word "across" was added to the page that contains other directional phrases.
- *Dynavox*: Joy uses a Dynavox to support her classroom communication. Sometimes, her soft voice and vocalizations are impossible for her classmates to hear. Her vocabulary on the Dynavox is also customized.
- *Printed copies of coordinate grids*: During the small group portion of this lesson, all students except Isadora used printed and laminated copies of coordinate grids. Isadora continued to work on the classroom iPad due to her fine motor issues.
- *Visual Magnification System (VMS)*: During the small group portion of this lesson, Joy worked on a VMS. She has limited vision, but can sometimes see and recognize lines, numbers, shapes and familiar images when they are enlarged.

## Progress Scale

Scales are used to track student progress for the entire week, not just for one lesson. The learning goal is always Level Three, so that there is always room for a Level Four assignment that makes sure the higher level students are challenged. At the beginning of this particular lesson, four students were already on Level Two (Steven, Tony, Joy and Carla) and two students were on Level One (Isadora and Bruce). Table 9.4 illustrates the Progress Scale used for this lesson.

Table 9.4 Progress Scale

Grade: MS Subject: Math Unit: 3—Points and Lines
Standards: MAFS.6.NS.3.AP.8a, MAFS.7.RP.1.AP.2a, MAFS.8.EE.3.AP.8a

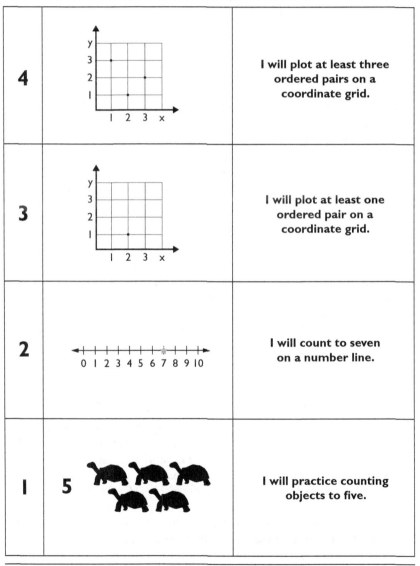

| 4 | | I will plot at least three ordered pairs on a coordinate grid. |
| 3 | | I will plot at least one ordered pair on a coordinate grid. |
| 2 | | I will count to seven on a number line. |
| 1 | | I will practice counting objects to five. |

## The Lesson: Perfect Pairs—Finding Animals on the Coordinate Plane

The lesson began by reviewing counting. Counting was Level One of the scale, and all six students had already reached that level of the scale the day before. The students love superheroes and cartoon drawings of superheroes found online were inserted to increase the interest level of the students. This review was quick: everyone had an opportunity to move two or three superheroes and, as they did, the Boardmaker program read the numbers and captions to them and the changing numbers were highlighted. Students complimented each other as they all completed the task.

### Whole Group

After the counting activity, the MimioStudio presentation began. The presentation came from the lesson sharing site, MimioConnect.com, and minor modifications were made. Level Two of the scale was counting on a number line, and Ms. K. needed to pay extra attention to Bruce and Isadora because they were the only two who had not demonstrated the skill and moved to Level Three. For this activity, Ms. K. moved the star to different numbers, then had all of the students practice counting until they reached the star. Joy counted verbally; Carla, Bruce, Steven and Tony used the numbers page on their TouchChat; and Isadora used the following simpler Boardmaker communication board on her iPad. While the TouchChat numbers page is rather complicated, it also has the numbers arranged sequentially. Students are expected to find the one, and follow along number by number with the teacher, and stop at the number the star is at. Both Bruce and Isadora were successful in this, so they were moved up to Level Two with their classmates.

The class then started on the learning goal: plotting an ordered pair on a coordinate plane. They practiced with the vocabulary words "across" and "up." Then Ms. K. demonstrated an example of plotting an ordered pair of animal pictures, drawing on the Mimio as she counted, then modeling checking her work. The next few examples were completed as a group. Ms. K. read the ordered pair, and the students instructed her to count across or up, and then the group counted together similar to what they did earlier along the number line. The students instructed Ms. K. to count the second number across or up, and they all counted the second number together. During this time, the paraprofessionals and teacher were providing the students with as many prompts as were needed, whether verbal, visual or gestural, for the students to be successful. However, the prompting was gradually faded, while still making sure the students were successful.

## Small Group

After the skill had been explicitly taught and practiced in the whole group, it was time to break into small groups. As the class transitioned, Ms. K. played one of the class' favorite counting songs on the board.

Transitioning can take a little while for Joy, because she has to move to the VMS. We also took this opportunity to get the materials for the small group. Isadora and Ms. K. were still working on the Mimio, but everyone else had their own laminated copies of the same coordinate grids, the same pictures and the same list of ordered pairs. These are illustrated in Figures 9.2, Ordered Pairs, and 9.3, Coordinate Grid.

*Figure 9.1* Ms. K. aids Steven in placing an ordered pair on his Coordinate Plane.

*Figure 9.2* Ordered Pairs.

Source: Reprinted with permission from Mimeo, LLC.

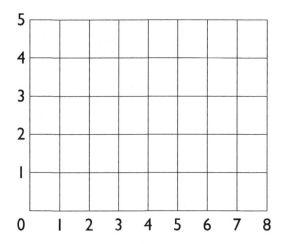

*Figure 9.3* Coordinate Grid.
Source: Reprinted with permission from Mimeo, LLC.

Twelve numbered pairs in total were given to each student, but most students were not able to practice with all twelve before the end of the lesson on this day. Figure 9.4 illustrates a completed Coordinate Grid.

During small group time, Ms. K. worked with Tony and Isadora, Miss. S. worked with Steven and Bruce, Carla's personal nurse worked with her and Mrs. M. worked with Joy, as she is Joy's specific paraprofessional. Figure 9.5 shows Tony focused on completing the activity independently.

**Plot these animals on the following points on the coordinate grid**

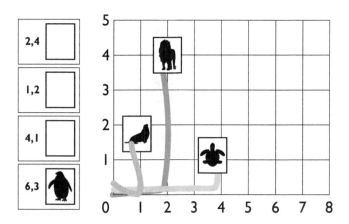

*Figure 9.4* Completed Coordinate Grid.
Source: Reprinted with permission by Mimio LLC.

*Figure 9.5* Tony works independently to place the zebra at 1, 1.

The class team worked with the students, giving them plenty of opportunities to practice, and fading prompts as they went. Figure 9.6 shows Carla working at the table with the grid and coordinates.

By the end of this particular day, Joy, Carla and Tony were all able to show mastery, and move up to Level Three of the scale. Joy was not able to move her pieces physically, but she was able to point and direct Mrs. M. about where they should go, as demonstrated in Figure 9.7, a photograph of Joy.

*Figure 9.6* Carla shows Nurse C. where she is placing her animals.

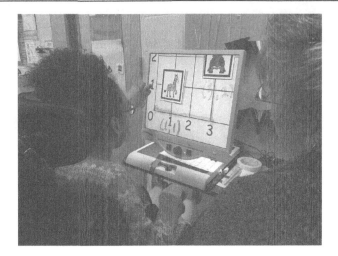

*Figure 9.7* Joy shows Mrs. M. the number 1 on the VMS.

Table 9.5 demonstrates how the personalized targets of the students were naturally integrated into the lesson. This shows that throughout the lesson, Ms. K. was able to meet the personal targets of all of the students except Tony. His focus was on the Access Points where he reached a Level Four on the Progress Chart.

## Reasons Ms. K. Believes This Was an Effective Lesson (This Section is Written in the First Person)

The school policy is always to make sure there are discrete tasks for every level of the scale and a learning goal that is demonstrable by the students. It looks different when different students complete the task. For example, Steven moves a piece of paper, Isadora drags on a computer screen and Joy gives verbal directions, but the task is achievable for all in personalized ways. For this particular lesson, Carla, Joy and Tony reached a Level Four, Steven and Bruce reached a Level Three, and Isadora reached a Level Two, making progress but falling short of the learning goal. Figure 9.8 shows Isadora working on the classroom iPad, interacting with a magnified version of the Coordinate Plane. The iPad is a portal of what is on the main screen, and it is zoomed in to the area she is working on.

In addition to the learning goal (or, as a support in aiding students in reaching the learning goal), the lesson was designed to feature practice in Math skills, for example, number recognition, one-to-one correspondence and counting (verbally or with the aid of a communication device). Some students just need a review, and some students have yet to master these

*Table 9.5* Personal Target Engagement

| Student | Targets | Review |
|---|---|---|
| Isadora | To use picture symbols to request the items needed to complete an academic or vocational task. | Isadora used her TouchChat to make the requests "I need iPad" when it was her turn to use the MimioMobile, and expressed through the AT "I need paper," when it was time to look at the printed worksheets. |
| Carla | To use a dynamic display device to answer an academic question within 10 seconds. | Carla was given the opportunity to answer questions on her AAC device. She was not successful during this lesson, but it afforded her an opportunity to practice and work on the skill. |
| | To use a dynamic display device to locate and select specific nouns. | Carla located the specific nouns of "turtle," "dog" and "mouse" using her TouchChat. |
| Joy | To ask or answer academic questions on her Dynavox. | Joy used her Dynavox to answer questions during this activity. Some answers she gave included "dog" and "turtle." She also used her Dynavox to say the numbers "2" and "4" in the activity where we were locating points on the coordinate grid. |
| | To use a variety of preprogrammed phrases on her Dynavox to interact with and direct others to complete routine-based classroom activities. | Joy used her Dynavox successfully to communicate to her peers "Good job" and "Try again." |
| Steve | To use a dynamic display device to locate specific adjectives and verbs. | Steve successfully used TouchChat to express the prepositions "across" and "up." This was an extension of his personal target. |
| Bruce | To use a dynamic display device to locate and select specific nouns. | Bruce located the specific nouns of "pig," "bird" and "mouse" using TouchChat. |
| Tony | None of Tony's personal targets were met in this lesson. His focus was on the Access Points where he reached a Level Four on the Progress Chart. | |

*Figure 9.8* Ms. K. holds the iPad so Isadora can check to see what animal will be at the ordered pair 3, 1.

skills. Even though Isadora did not meet the learning goal this time around, she still received exposure to the concepts, was able to review her numbers and demonstrated the ability to count to seven on a number line, a skill that we have been working on all year. Students were encouraged to interact with each other, calling each other by name and giving feedback on their responses. I feel that any lesson can be a good lesson if you can make the students positive during it and foster positive interactions, no matter what the subject matter is.

This lesson was successful in keeping the students engaged. In addition to maintaining a positive voice and adding little high interest touches to the lesson, such as the transition video and the use of the superhero cartoon pictures, I also made sure to keep the students on task, not only during small group, but whole group as well. Most of the times when I was counting on the board, the students were counting along, and both the paraprofessionals and teacher were vigilant, making sure everyone was on task and that they had the support they needed to participate. When individual students were demonstrating skills during whole group, the other students were also paying attention, both because they were expected to give feedback to their friends, but also so they could know what kind of feedback to give ("Awesome job," "Try again," "I can help you with that," etc.) The classroom team expects everyone to participate, therefore they keep an eye on everyone and provide prompts when needed. For the small group, everyone had their own personal grid to work on, so there was also a lack of downtime, or time for them to get distracted. This focus on student engagement not only improves their learning, but reduces behavior issues as well.

Individualization is always key, and it is impossible to do that without really knowing your students. Take time with them, pay attention to their levels and their strengths and their idiosyncrasies. Study over their IEPs. Students are always changing, so make sure to keep reassessing and reevaluating in your mind. Knowing your students, you can create the necessary achievable tasks for whichever lesson you are working on. In some cases, this might mean changing a pencil and paper activity to one on the computer, or changing an activity where you are supposed to create something into one where you are describing what should be created.

For example, if the learning goal you are working on is "Create a model of an ecosystem," a student who is physically incapable of completing the task might be given the opportunity to choose an ecosystem ("ocean") and tell what a model of it might contain ("fish, shark, seaweed"). You can still do the creation task with them hand-over-hand if you wish, but you would assess them on, and let them show off, their knowledge with an achievable task. In other cases, creating achievable tasks for a student might require simplification of the learning goal. High expectations are desirable for all students, but there is no reason to go over their heads in a way that will be meaningless to them.

In the beginning parts of this lesson, Direct Instruction was employed. It was kept relatively short and direct, as I did not want to lose the students' attention. However, in this lesson, it proved beneficial to teach explicitly exactly what it looks like when you plot coordinate pairs. I included a lot of repetition and time for practice. I believe Math skills generally need a lot of practice for mastery. This lesson had 12 different coordinate pairs, and 12 different animal pictures. Each practice was slightly different (and students could not complete the task through memorization), but the skill itself was repeated a lot.

The level of support changed as the lesson progressed and the Prompting Hierarchy was employed. Do not give the students choices or help that they do not need, let them show what they know. It goes along with having High Expectations. Students are always growing and changing, and if the support they have needed in the past is provided without thinking about it, the students will not be able to show what they can do.

For this particular lesson, every student did need full prompting at the beginning—it was a brand new skill, and I wanted each one to participate and feel some success while learning the new skill. However, the classroom team were careful to fade the prompts and waited until they were sure the student needed the support for each step before providing it. The last strategy used was Flexible Groupings for the small groups. I am always careful when putting groups together, balancing personality differences, learning styles and knowing which students can work more independently in a group, as opposed to those who need more teacher attention. I acknowledge the groups in this lesson worked well, with no issues.

# Chapter 10

# "It's in the Bag"— Using Measurement to Decorate Shopping Bags

*With Helen Pastore*

This lesson takes place at Spring Park School, in the TRANSITION 9–12+ team.

## The Classroom

There are nine students in the classroom. The students are impacted by multiple exceptionalities, including Intellectual Disability (InD), orthopedic, neurological and medical issues, Autism Spectrum Disorder (ASD), and sometimes they also have mental health issues. One student uses a manual wheelchair and another uses a power wheelchair, while all the remaining students can walk independently. Communication is encouraged through spoken and sign language as well as Alternative Augmentative Communication (AAC), for example TouchChat, Proloquo2Go on iPads and a Dynavox. Standardized assessments, behavior data and evaluations, including students' self-monitoring materials, are used to guide and inform instruction. Progress monitoring indicates when a student needs less support or additional strategies to support their movement towards agreed annual goals. The student's performance also informs the teacher when the student is not yet able to complete the task independently, indicating a need to increase explicit instruction or to modify strategies. Direct and indirect instruction across the class provides a balance of whole group, small group and one-on-one activities supported by classroom paraprofessionals. The curriculum follows the standard course descriptions presented by the state Department of Education for Exceptional Student Education (ESE), specifically the state Standard Access Points. Mrs. P. selects materials in alignment with the curriculum and each student's Individual Education Plan (IEP).

## The Adults

Mrs. P. is in her eleventh year of teaching. She graduated with a Bachelor of Science in Education (Recreation Education) in 1976 from Northeastern

University. After a previous career, she entered the teaching profession in 2005 and completed an Alternate Certification program during her first year of teaching. Her certifications are ESE K-12, Elementary K-6, Severe Endorsement, Reading Endorsement and ASD Endorsement. She completed a Master of Arts ASD and InD at USF in 2013. She was a teacher of students with emotional/behavioral challenges for 2 years. Since then she has been a teacher of middle, high and post-high school students with complex learning needs. She has served in a variety of leadership roles within and outside the school, including Team Leader, Community of Practice and a writing committee member for Access Points. Mr. H. joined this class 5 years ago as a paraprofessional after many years on the Security team at a local middle school. He received a Bachelor of Science in Music Education in the 1970s. Mrs. S. came to this class as a paraprofessional to supplement classroom staff in support of students with severe behavioral challenges. She earned her Bachelor of Science in Mathematics several years ago and began raising her family before joining this class. Mrs. W. is new to the class this year as a paraprofessional. She has worked with students with complex needs since the early years of this school's formation about 30 years ago.

Integral to the classroom staff are teams of therapeutic staff identified on specific students' IEPs. Teams include a speech and language pathologist, an occupational therapist, consultation with a physical therapist and members of a Local Assistive Technology Service (LATS) staff.

## The Students

All the students in this class have an annual IEP with goals in the domains of Curriculum & Learning, Social/Emotional, Independent Functioning and Communication. All students are eligible and receive specialized transportation and have regularly scheduled community-based instruction experiences, as well as engagement in a specially designed campus-based work center and other campus-based work experiences. Post-school plans for these students are likely to result in placement at adult learning centers where they can continue to receive instruction in adult daily living and pre-employability skills development. Some have been in this group for multiple years and some are relative newcomers.

JoJo is identified under the disability category of Intellectual Disability (InD). She uses spoken language and can read and write at 2nd Grade level. Her previous class was deemed to be too challenging with regard to social expectations, which was particularly concerning because that class went off-campus to a work site twice per week. She enjoys work tasks and is quite responsive to others whom she can help in some way. When she is feeling overwhelmed she will not speak and will decline participation in learning activities. Having recently joined this class, she has begun interacting with classmates who use TouchChat and Dynavox programs. Her daily instructional goals (emerging from her IEP), addressed in this lesson, are:

- Curriculum and Learning: to count real-world objects into groups up to 10.
- Independent Functioning: to follow a model to complete a multi-step task.

Billy uses a speech-generating device and sign language as his primary mode of communication and is identified under the disability categories of Intellectual Disability (InD) and Autism Spectrum Disorder (ASD). His AAC is a mini-iPad that is organized with labeled pictorial folders. Within each category, he can scroll to the specific item and create sentences to express his wants, needs and feelings. There is a file for jokes to share with friends, which enhances social and communication experiences, especially for peers who are fearful of his very aggressive behaviors. While his preference to work alone is well established, increased use of his device has begun to expand his self-confidence in relating to others. In addition to a diagnosis of intellectual disability and ASD, he also has medical issues and Visual Impairment (VI). As a result, he draws objects close to his eye and seems to need a color format to best interpret his environment. He exhibits issues with fine motor skills. His behavioral plan is designed for increasing positive social interactions with his peers and decreasing aggression towards others, particularly authority figures. His daily instructional goals (emerging from his IEP), addressed in this lesson, are:

- Curriculum and Learning: to count real-world objects into groups up to 10.
- Communication: to use his AAC device to create a message as part of a thank you note.

Lin has a primary diagnosis of Autism Spectrum Disorder (ASD) and is identified under the disability category of Intellectual Disability (InD). She moved to a group home when her mother became seriously ill and recently enrolled at Spring Park School. Intellectually, she performs Math and reading activities at an upper elementary grade level. She speaks at a very quick tempo with very low volume. She prefers Math and reading activities over other tasks. Nonetheless, she masters multi-step work tasks with relative ease and can stay on task with occasional verbal prompting. She shows signs of recovery from depression and initiates light hugs with staff to whom she feels a comfortable connection. She is bilingual, in English and Korean. She tends to walk very slowly with eyes closed and feels annoyed when staff gently prompt her to keep her eyes open and engage in activities. Her daily instructional goal (emerging from her IEP), addressed in this lesson, is:

- Independent Functioning: to engage in a task within 20 seconds of being directed to begin by an adult.

Mark has been in this class since 6th Grade. He is very social and is well known on campus. His learning needs are impacted by Intellectual Disability (InD), a medical condition, orthopedic factors and Speech and Language Impairment (SLI). Because he can carry on a simple conversation, he is thought to be intellectually higher than he can actually perform, which appears to hover around the pre-K–1st Grade level. He struggles to comprehend abstract concepts, however he enjoys following pictorial directions to complete tasks. Recently he was able to complete a three-dimensional puzzle of an animal, with support to identify puzzle pieces from an illustration and to stay on a given step. He uses a wheelchair independently and responds favorably to simple verbal direction. His is bilingual, in Spanish and English. His daily instructional goal (emerging from his IEP), addressed in this lesson, is:

- Curriculum and Learning: to count real-world objects into groups up to 10.

Sadie is new to this class, coming from a local general educational setting. She is identified under the disability category of Intellectual Disability (InD). She is social and uses her Dynavox and cross-scanner independently. Due to neurological and physical disabilities, she requires full assistance for meeting her personal needs. She navigates with reasonable ease by power wheelchair and can instruct staff in the use of her lift when she needs to be transferred out of her chair. Cognitively intact at about the 2nd Grade level in all areas, Sadie is now consciously struggling with her need to self-advocate. Her goal is to go to college. Her daily instructional goals (emerging from her IEP), addressed in this lesson, are:

- Curriculum and Learning: to locate and retrieve materials needed to complete a work task.
- Communication: to use her AAC device to create a message as part of a thank you note.

Jim has been a member of this class for several years and is identified under the disability category of Intellectual Disability (InD). He has made very good progress in the area of social skills. When he first came to class he would lay down on the floor at the end of the hallway and refuse to come into the room. While he still occasionally sits on the floor, he is more likely than not to re-join the group with a verbal or physical prompt of an outstretched hand for him to grasp. He has also improved his communication from shriek-like speech to a "young man's voice." He will use one or two spoken words for requests or responses on occasion. He is quite sensitive to loud, unexpected noises, at which point he will separate himself from the group. He eats soft or pureed food. He prefers to move around the room, sometimes at a slow trot or dancing. At those times he often invites others to join him. When he is sitting, he is often singing or asking for songs and acting as a conductor of an orchestra with his hands moving to the music he must be hearing in his head. His fine motor is limited and he receives occupational therapy services. Intellectually, he appears to perform within the range of Kindergarten to 2nd Grade with support and guidance. His daily instructional goals (emerging from his IEP), addressed in this lesson, are:

- Curriculum and Learning: to use rulers, thermometers and other tools to measure common objects.
- Social/Emotional: to engage in a task within 20 seconds of being directed to begin.

Mike is identified under the disability category of Intellectual Disability (InD) and is new to the class. Due to medical issues, he is on a special diet. He walks with an awkward gait and receives occupational therapy services to support fine motor skills. He speaks with a loud voice and uses simple, complete sentences. He has excellent manners and very much wants to please; he likes to be part of the group. He has distracting behaviors such as loud hand clapping and nonsensical vocalization. Intellectually, he appears to be performing at a pre-Kindergarten level. He appears to learn by rote and he struggles to distinguish the essence of a thought or idea; as a result, he is often close but not on topic. His daily instructional goals (emerging from his IEP), addressed in this lesson, are:

- Curriculum and Learning: to count real-world objects into groups up to 10.
- Communication: to respond to "Yes/No" questions using picture/ word cards and respond to questions in short sentences.
- Independent Functioning: to locate and retrieve materials needed to complete a work task.

Star transferred to Spring Park School 3 years ago and has enjoyed a tremendous reduction of anxiety. She is identified under the disability categories of Intellectual Disability (InD) and Autism Spectrum Disorder (ASD). While she speaks with perfect diction, she generally uses a simple and familiar phrase to declare her need (such as "Go to the bathroom"). She is fluent with her Proloquo2Go program on her personal iPad and used it in communication when she first enrolled in our school. However, as her anxiety decreased, so did her willingness to use her communication in the school setting. The family has found that she will still use communication during times of great distress. Intellectually, she appears to perform at a mid to upper elementary level. She is bilingual, in Hindi and English. Her daily instructional goals (emerging from her IEP), addressed in this lesson, are:

- Curriculum and Learning: to use rulers, thermometers and other tools to measure common objects.
- Social/Emotional: to follow a model to complete a multi-step task.
- Communication: to use her AAC device to create a message as part of a thank you note.

George recently enrolled in the school following a move from another county prompted by a parent's terminal illness. He is identified under the disability categories of Intellectual Disability (InD) and Autism Spectrum Disorder (ASD). He is beginning to use an iPad with TouchChat and is being evaluated for the most suitable device through a Local Assistive Technology Service (LATS) evaluation. His vocal output is composed of guttural sounds. However, his receptive skills are more developed and he responds well to others socially. During an academic assignment he often interrupts his work to go to another part of the room and put away objects that others have left out of place (even if the other person may be using the items). He likes to participate in most activities, particularly if they involve the use of a laptop or cooking. His daily instructional goals (emerging from his IEP), addressed in this lesson, are:

- Curriculum and Learning: to use rulers, thermometers and other tools to measure common objects.
- Communication: to use his AAC device to create a message as part of a thank you note.

## Overview of Lesson

This is a Math lesson that uses measurement in a real-world application. Students learn how Math is used to produce a product for a local yarn store. The lesson incorporates a variety of technology and measurement strategies. The product is a retail shopping bag for customer purchase. The bag is decorated with two labels and yarn, counted and bundled into groups of 10. For select students an extended task can be added to engage them in calculating the volume of yarn and supplies that can fit into each size bag. Over the course of the school year, each student performs a multi-step task.

### Long-term Planning

The annual scope in this year's Math course encompasses algebra, geometry, numbers and quantity, interpreting data and solving problems. Table 10.1 illustrates the differentiated skills in the long-term planning at Spring Park School. This lesson addresses measurement standards within geometry.

*Table 10.1* Long-term Planning: Differentiated Skills at Spring Park School

| Independently Functioning Students will... | Supported Students will... | Participatory Students will... |
|---|---|---|
| • Demonstrate the use of tools for Math concepts and problem solving.<br>• Complete Math tasks independently, including initiating tasks and engaging in discussion on topic. | • Select pictures with text to complete Math problems.<br>• Identify tools used to solve Math problems, such as rulers and scales and counting jigs.<br>• Follow models to use Math tools. | • Given errorless choices of pictures and on AAC devices, make a selection to communicate facts related to Math.<br>• Accept physical prompts to complete Math tasks.<br>• Recognize purpose of counting/sorting jigs. |

### Medium-term Planning

The unit on measurement is scheduled in the second marking period of the first semester. It includes Math vocabulary development as well as hands-on activities about length, liquid and weight measurements. This is illustrated in Table 10.2.

### Short-term Planning

This lesson on length and quantity takes place over the course of a week and this particular one occurs on Tuesday. Table 10.3 illustrates how it fits in with the Math lessons across the week. During this lesson, students measure and count real objects using materials to create a retail product.

The Access Points that this lesson engages in are:

- MAFS.912.G-CO.1—Identify precise definition of angle, circle, perpendicular line, parallel line and line segment, based on the undefined notions of point, line, distance along a line and distance around a circular arc.
- Objectives—Students will recognize and define the length of a segment by measuring yarn, the bag and label, and locate the center of the bag for label placement using a completed sample for comparison.

Differentiation and increased complexity are provided for Star, Lin and JoJo by applying an additional Math standard:

- MAFS.912.G-MG.1.2—Apply concepts of density based on area and volume in modeling situations.
- Objectives—Students will measure the dimensions of a bag and apply the formula to calculate volume, using calculators as needed.

*Table 10.2* Medium-term Math Planning at Spring Park School

| Objectives |
| --- |
| Students will use a systematic approach to plan steps within a task by listing and sequencing the steps of the task. |
| Students will follow a sequence of steps to locate and gather materials to create a decorated shopping bag. |
| Students will use individual modes of communication to request assistance, such as "Will you help me measure this side?" |

*Table 10.3* Short-term Planning

| Day | Objective |
| --- | --- |
| Monday | Recognize, identify and group objects used in the task of decorating bags. |
| Tuesday | Demonstrate the use of rulers and scissors by measuring and cutting lengths of yarn and organizing bags into groups of 10. |
| Wednesday | Apply adhesive business partner label to the back of each bag. |
| Thursday | Apply yarn bits onto a bag and adhere the adhesive logo label on each bag front. |
| Friday | Using pre-measured length of yarn, tie together bags grouped in tens and place in a shipping carton, then calculate final total of completed bags. |

### Personal Learning Objectives

Lin, Mark, Jim, Mike and JoJo are expected to use spoken language throughout the lesson. In particular, Jim and Mike respond to "Yes/No" questions using picture/word cards and short sentences and use their words to ask for materials. JoJo is provided with script prompts to support her speaking. For example, a written sentence such as "I need help with the next step" is coupled with her pointing to a visual schedule that identifies the tasks within a multi-step activity.

Star, George, Sadie and Billy will use their personal communication devices. Star will upload a visual schedule of the tasks that she needs to complete during the activity. Within partnered communication, Star uses her device to announce her completion of each task and identify her next task or request help. With one-to-one assistance, George navigates his device to make requests for more materials and respond to questions in sentence form, such as "Yes, I need more yarn" rather than "Yes." He will copy a script to create a thank you note at the end of the lesson. Billy will be supported to use his device to count by verbal prompts. On his device there is a file with numbers and he will be directed to open the file and name each number as he counts 10 bags. To support Mike in counting real-world objects (bags) into groups up to 10, a jig will be provided. The jig is a series of cup hooks adhered to a wall with each hook being labeled 1–10 with enough space to hang a bag on each hook to learn one-to-one correspondence.

*Materials Provided by Retail Yarn Store*

- Carton of white paper bags.
- Printed adhesive labels with company logo for the front of the bags.
- Printed ("business partner") adhesive labels for the back of the bags.
- Generous supply of colorful yarn cuttings (about 3 inches in length).
- A skein of yarn to be cut by students into 18-inch lengths (for tying bundles of bags).

### Resources Used in the Lesson

The resources used were ActivBoard and iPads equipped with TouchChat, Proloquo2Go and Internet access. Work tables were arranged for task differentiation: one for blank bags, one for adhering back labels only, one for adhering front labels only and one for bags that need to be bundled and tied. A jig for counting bags into sets of 10 (numbered hooks adhered to a wall) was used, as well as a document camera, scissors, rulers and sample bag.

## The Lesson: "It's in the Bag": Using Measurement to Decorate Shopping Bags

Students identify the length and width of the shopping bag, length of yarn and logo sticker. They decorate the bags by measuring lengths of yarn, which are placed on the bag and secured by the label. Students locate the center of the bag, where the yarn and label are affixed. Prior to this specific lesson, students viewed a YouTube video titled "Introduction to Standard Measurement for Kids: Measuring Length in Inches with a Ruler," which demonstrates the skill of using a ruler. Further, a video called "Salespersons," which contains images of work tasks at business locations, was viewed in the Safari Montage library. This was shown to provide background information as students prepare for a future beyond school. Safari Montage is an application provided by the school district and may not be an available resource in all schools. This was to establish an understanding that a retail business has products to sell and customers need to carry their purchases home. Mrs. P. emphasizes the students' role in creating a product (decorated shopping bags) as part of a business cycle. The students also visit the yarn store, meet the business owner, see that customers like the bags and how the employees store and retrieve the bags. They see that the staff appreciate their work and that they, the students, provide a valuable service to the yarn store. Students use communication devices, picture/words and spoken/written words to write a descriptive article for the school newsletter as a post-activity task. The writing tasks meet other curricula and IEP goals in student preparation for post-school living. These activities coordinate and align with other standards and goals within the students' overall schedule of courses.

### *Whole Group Work*

Mrs. P. presents the company website on the ActivBoard and conducts review questions about the task. These include:

- Who are we performing the work for?
- Who is the consumer?
- Why do consumers need shopping bags?
- How many bags did the company send for us to decorate? (Students locate information on carton.)
- How many bags will be counted into bundles?

The students use a model shopping bag to measure the length of each side of the bag, measure the size of the label and measure for the placement of the label when secured to the bag. A jig or a ruler is available for students to use. Each student will measure and cut 18-inch lengths of yarn (about 25 pieces).

*Figure 10.1* Measuring a length of yarn for tying.

## Individual Work

The sequence of the tasks assigned to individual students across the group is:

1    Retrieve supplies and place on designated tables.
2    Locate laminated personal checklist to monitor progress.
3    Adhere back label to the bag at the assigned table. *In order to do this, the students place a bag with the back facing up and, using a sample as a model, locate the corresponding place on the blank bag. They then pull a "partner" label from the adhesive sheet and place it on the blank bag. Once this is complete, they move the completed bag to the side and retrieve another blank bag.*

*Figure 10.2* Measuring length of bag.

4    At the assigned table adhere front label to the bag. *In order to do this, the students place a bag with the front side facing up and, using a sample as a model, locate the corresponding place on the blank bag. They then grasp a few yarn scraps and sprinkle them on the face of the bag, pull a "logo" label from the adhesive sheet and place it on the yarn, such that the edges of the yarn project from under the label, and secure the edges of the label firmly to the bag. Once this is complete, they move the completed bag to the side and retrieve another blank bag.*
5    Completed bags are placed on a counting jig or the student counts 10 bags and gives these to a fellow student who will use yarn to tie into bundles of 10 bags.
6    Bundles of completed bags are placed into a box carton.

At each step, students use their communication system with staff support as needed. For example, "Star, I need more labels, please," "Here are 10 bags, Mike," "This bag is 8 inches tall and 12 inches wide," "This yarn is soft," "This piece is blue," etc.

As students repeat the tasks they perfect their measuring skills and develop fluency with their communication systems and speech through frequent interaction with peers. Assigning different roles within the project, which also serves to maintain student engagement, creates novel opportunities. For example, on one day Mike may measure 18-inch lengths of yarn and on another day count bags into bundles of 10. Students will have a changing pattern of language and vocabulary because their roles and tasks are changed.

This lesson is repeated across the school year to meet students' needs to have repetitive learning opportunities to fulfill curriculum goals and support IEP goals in gaining competence in communication, social and independent functioning skills. Tasks are completed with one-on-one guidance and paired cooperation. For example, Jim will ask George for a ruler and George will use his AAC device to say "Here is a ruler" and give Jim the ruler. Jim may need hand-over-hand assistance from an adult to use the ruler. To some extent the opportunities to provide support vary throughout the activity, requiring adults to recognize those opportunities and maximize cooperative experiences between students. Assessments include formative and summative, using rubrics and checklists that integrate IEP goals and activity participation for each component of the unit. Table 10.4 demonstrates the personal target engagement the students achieved in the lesson and demonstrates how Mrs. P. was able to integrate personal targets into the lesson.

*Figure 10.3* Measuring width of bag.

*Table 10.4* Personal Target Engagement

| Student | Targets | Review |
|---------|---------|--------|
| JoJo | To count real-world objects into groups up to 10. | JoJo counted groups of 10 bags from a stack and tied them together before placing in the shipping cart. |
| | To follow a model to complete a multi-step task. | JoJo followed a simple written checklist of three steps for logo placement on the back of a bag. |
| Billy | To count real-world objects into groups up to 10. | Billy placed individual bags on the 10 numbered coat hook jig and verbally counted 1–10 (with verbal prompting). |
| | To use his AAC device to create a message as part of a thank you note. | Billy used TouchChat to copy a "Thank you" message to the yarn store. |
| Lin | To engage in a task within 20 seconds of being directed to begin by an adult. | An adult verbally prompted Lin to retrieve and store task materials. |
| Mark | To count real-world objects into groups up to 10. | Mark placed individual bags on the 10 numbered coat hook jig and verbally counted 1–10 (with verbal prompting). |
| Sadie | To locate and retrieve materials needed to complete a work task. | An adult verbally prompted Sadie to retrieve and store task materials and prompted follow through by Sadie. |
| | To use her AAC device to create a message as part of a thank you note. | Sadie used a model to create her own "Thank you" message using her Dynavox. |
| Jim | To use rulers, thermometers and other tools to measure common objects. | Jim used the ruler to measure the yarn (with physical prompting). |
| | To engage in a task within 20 seconds of being directed to begin. | An adult verbally prompted Jim to maintain measuring yarn task completion. |

| Mike | To count real-world objects into groups up to 10. | Mike placed individual bags on the 10 numbered coat hook jig and verbally counted 1–10 (with verbal prompting). |
|---|---|---|
| | To respond to yes/no questions using picture/word cards and respond to questions in short sentences. | Mike successfully responded to direct short questions about what he was actually doing in the measuring task. |
| | To locate and retrieve materials needed to complete a work task. | An adult verbally prompted Mike to retrieve and store task materials and prompted follow through. |
| Star | To use rulers, thermometers and other tools to measure common objects. | Star followed a verbal prompt to locate a measuring tool (ruler) to measure the bags for logo placement. |
| | To follow a model to complete a multi-step task. | Star followed a simple written checklist of five steps for logo placement on back and front of bag. |
| | To use her AAC device to create a message as part of a thank you note. | Star used Proloquo2Go to create her own message, "Thank you," to the owner of the yarn store. |
| George | To use rulers, thermometers and other tools to measure common objects. | George used a ruler to measure labels, bags and yarn. |
| | To use his AAC device to create a message as part of a thank you note. | George used TouchChat to create his own message to the owner of the yarn store. |

## Reasons Mrs. P. Believes This Was an Effective Lesson (This Section is Written in the First Person)

I believe measuring student learning and progress is fundamental to instruction. I developed a student checklist of skills for this lesson, which informed future instruction. For example, a checklist was used to monitor a particular student's ability to count to 10, to track the level of prompting a student required to be successful and to collect data on the frequency of using a communication device. I believe this to be an efficient progress monitoring process.

The "bag job" project has become a favorite for many reasons. There is something for everyone in this lesson. It is a real-world job that has connected the class with a local retail business. The owner loves meeting the students and that they fulfill a task in the business that her staff prefers not to do. She relates the story of the relationship with the school to her customers with glee, and the customers are endeared to the initiative to engage students within society. The multiple components of the learning activity can cross academic standards content areas and IEP goals. Students progress from needing continual adult assistance to being able to perform every step of the project. Independently. The practical application of measuring has a real-world connection with a tangible product. It also challenges students with higher order thinking about comparing actual outcomes with predictions. For example, students develop interpersonal and collaborative skills as communication is required to complete the activity: students must ask each other for materials as needed, remind each other that 10 bags make a bundle and so on. Through email, students contact the store owner to inquire about the next delivery of bags and whether the work quality is satisfactory, further generalizing communication skills. Students are rightfully proud of their success, and other teachers in the school have noticed and commented on the enterprise. This school acknowledgement generates excitement and energy about the lesson, which helps students reflect on the success when tackling unfamiliar or non-preferred tasks.

Engagement is ensured as the paraprofessionals and I support each student by direct assistance (such as hand-over-hand) and partnered communication. Student tasks are juggled to expand skills development. For example, adhering back labels is one step whereas adhering front labels involves several steps. In this way, higher level comprehension and a level of abstract thinking is encouraged. The lesson allows an active response to certain sensory needs. For example, a kinesthetic learner may prefer moving bags from place to place rather than touching the yarn. While this lesson is very hands-on, I believe there are many ways to engage students across curricular content areas. For instance, a lesson about money can be used to practice monetary exchange. A group web search can explore where various wool-producing animals live and how plants are used to produce fabric as an activity pertaining to the classification of living things. In my experience, the lesson is easily generalized. For example, using similar steps, "goodie bags" or gift bags can be created with appropriate decorations. Such products might be a fundraising activity for a class to fund community-based instruction or replenish classroom supplies.

Creating appropriate lesson plans is an ongoing challenge because of the importance of meeting students "where they are" and moving them forward in their learning. IEP goals need to be balanced with standard curriculum demands. Student learning behaviors need to be supported and contribute to the advancement of social skills. Preparing students to transition to post-school education and training is a complex process and using a community driven activity allows the students to experience life out of school.

For this lesson, I relied on the lesson preparation site: www.accesstofls. weebly.com for information under headings Instructional Resource Guide, Instructional Families, UDL Units Math Resources by Course and MASSIs. These resources help to connect state Access Points to the General Education Standards in meaningful ways for each of the students' IEP goals, communication needs and learning styles. Specific instructional strategies that I utilized in this lesson included accessing prior knowledge about using numbers. As part of direct instruction, we counted in unison as I pointed to each number on a number line that was displayed on the ActivBoard. Conspicuous strategies are very useful. For students who do not have 1:1 correspondence the students practiced counting while touching each number. Explicit instruction is important. I do not want to assume knowledge that a student may not have developed, so each component is "spelled out." This included a "*how to* video" to supplement hand-over-hand support for skill development. However I do assume each student can learn the lesson's objectives. I use modeling, guided practice and a prompt hierarchy that moves each student towards concept mastery and task completion as independently as possible. Using data (progress monitoring via a skill checklist in this lesson), I will modify a task as needed. An obvious example for an emerging communicator is prompting the use of the AAC device. The concrete "counting jig" was successful to support the concept that counting has a purpose; in this lesson the purpose is to group the bags into a manageable amount to secure with a length of yarn.

Another strategy seen in this lesson is allowing "adequate time." While adequate time does relate to pacing the activity so as not to rush the process, the more valuable idea for the student is to repeat the concept of measuring length in many ways. In just this lesson several items are measured (the sides of the bag, the sides of the label and the yarn to be used to tie bundles). As additional practice, we also measure tables, doors and various items across campus to make connections about how measurement is used in daily life. In a different direction, we do cooking activities that use different measurements, e.g., the size of pans and pots, the volume of liquids and the quantity of place settings. Additionally, using the approach of "I do, we do together, you do" is a critical strategy in identifying what the student can and cannot do, what point is problematic for the student and what point is a source of righteous pride when the student succeeds.

# References

Allday, R. A., Neilsen-Gatti, S., & Hudson, T. M. (2013). Preparation for inclusion in teacher education pre-service curricula. *Teacher Education and Special Education: The Journal of the Teacher Education Division of the Council for Exceptional Children*, 36(4), 298–311.

Althoff, R. R., Kuny-Slock, A. V., Verhulst, F. C., Hudziak, J. J., & van der Ende, J. (2014). Classes of oppositional-defiant behavior: Concurrent and predictive validity. *Journal of Child Psychology and Psychiatry*, 55(10), 1162–1171.

Americans with Disabilities Act of 1990, Pub. L. No. 101–336, 104 Stat. 328 (1990).

Ayres, K. M., Lowrey, K. A., Douglas, K. H., & Sievers, C. (2011). I can identify Saturn but I can't brush my teeth: What happens when the curricular focus for students with severe disabilities shifts. *Education and Training in Autism and Developmental Disabilities*, 46, 11–21.

Ayres, K., Mechling, L., & Sansosti, F. (2013). The use of mobile technologies to assist with life skills/independence of students with moderate/severe intellectual disability and/or autism spectrum disorders: Considerations for the future of school psychology. *Psychology in the Schools*, 50(3), 259–271.

Baglieri, S., & Knopf, J. H. (2004). Normalizing difference in inclusive teaching. *Journal of Learning Disabilities*, 37(6), 525–529.

Bambara, L. M., Koger, F., & Bartholomew, A. (2011). Building skills for home and community. In M. E. Snell & F. Brown (Eds.), *Instruction of students with severe disabilities* (7th ed., pp. 529–569). Upper Saddle River, NJ: Pearson.

Beech, M., McKay, J., Barnitt, V., & Orlando, C. (2002). *Dealing with differences: Accommodations that work!* Trainer manual. Tallahassee: Florida Department of Education, Bureau of Exceptional Education and Student Services.

Bellini, S., Peters, J. K., & Benner, L. (2007). A meta-analysis of school-based social skills interventions for children with autism spectrum disorders. *Remedial & Special Education*, 28(3), 153–162.

Bethune, K., & Wood, C. (2013). Effects of coaching on teachers' use of function-based interventions for students with severe disabilities. *Teacher Education and Special Education*, 36(2), 97–114.

Biklen, D., & Burke, J. (2006). Presuming competence. *Equity & Excellence in Education*, 39(2), 166–175.

Browder, D., Ahlgrim-Delzell, L., Spooner, F., Mims, P. J., & Baker, J. (2009). Using time delay to teach literacy to students with severe developmental disabilities. *Exceptional Children*, 75, 343–364.

Browder, D. M., Spooner, F., Algozzine, R., Ahlgrim-Delzell, L., Flowers, C., & Karvonen, M. (2003). What we know and need to know about alternate assessment. *Exceptional Children*, 1, 45.

Browder, D. M., Wakeman, S. Y., & Flowers, C. (2007). Creating access to the general curriculum with links to grade-level content for students with significant cognitive disabilities: An explication of the concept. *The Journal of Special Education*, 41(1), 2–16.

Browder, D. M., Wakeman, S. Y., Spooner, F., Ahlgrim-Delzell, L., & Algozzine, B. (2006). Research on reading instruction for individuals with significant cognitive disabilities. *Exceptional Children*, 72(4), 392–408.

Browder, D. M., Wood, L., Thompson, J., & Ribuffo, C. (2014). Evidence-based practices for students with severe disabilities (document no. IC-3). Retrieved from University of Florida, Collaboration for Effective Educator, Development, Accountability, and Reform Center website: http://ceedar. education.ufl.edu/wp-content/uploads/2014/09/IC-3_FINAL_03-03-15.pdf

Bunning, K. (2009). Making sense of communication. In J. Pawlyn & S. Carnaby (Eds.), *Profound intellectual and multiple disabilities: Nursing complex needs* (pp. 46–61). London: Wiley-Blackwell.

Byers, R., & Lawson, H. (2015). Priorities, products and process: Developments in providing curriculum for learners with SLD/PMLD. In P. Lacey, R. Ashdown, P. Jones, H. Lawson & M. Pipe (Eds.), *The Routledge companion to severe, profound and multiple learning difficulties* (pp. 38–48). London: Routledge.

Carpenter, B., Egerton, J., Cockbill, B., Bloom, T., Fotheringham, J., & Rawson, H. (2015). *Engaging learners with complex learning difficulties and disabilities*. London: Routledge.

Carpenter, B., Rose, S., Rawson, J., & Egerton, J. (2011). *The rules of engagement: Special education needs*. Retrieved from https://senmagazine.co.uk (accessed November 18, 2016).

Chaturvedi, A., Murdick, N. L., & Gartin, B. C. (2014). Obsessive compulsive disorder: What an educator needs to know. *Physical Disabilities: Education and Related Services*, 33(2), 71–83.

Collins, B., Kleinert, H., & Land, L. (2006). Addressing math standards and functional math. In D. Browder & F. Spooner (Eds.), *Teaching language arts, math and science to students with significant cognitive disabilities* (pp. 197–228). Baltimore, MD: Paul Brookes.

Copeland, S. R., & Cosbey, J. (2010). Making progress in the general curriculum: Rethinking effective instructional practices. *Research and Practice for Persons with Severe Disabilities*, 33, 214–227.

Courtade, G., Spooner, F., Browder, D. M., & Jimenez, B. (2012). Seven reasons to teach promote standards-based instruction for students with severe disabilities. *Education and Training in Autism and Developmental Disabilities*, 47, 3–13.

Dahle, K. B. (2003). Services to include young children with autism in the general classroom. *Early Childhood Special Education*, 31(1), 65–70.

Desai, T., Chow, K., Mumford, L., Hotze, F., & Chau, T. (2014). Implementing an iPad-based alternative communication device for a student with cerebral palsy and autism in the classroom via an access technology delivery protocol. *Computers & Education*, 79, 148–158.

Donnellan, A. (1984). The criterion of the least dangerous assumption. *Behavioral Disorders*, 9, 141–150.

Education for all Handicapped Children Act. (1975). In A. Lerner, B. Lerner, & K. Lee Lerner (Eds.), *Human and civil rights: Essential primary sources* (pp. 459–462). Detroit: Gale, 2006.

Engagement Profile and Scale. Retrieved from http://complexld.ssatrust.org.uk/project-resources/engagement-profile-scale.html (accessed November 18, 2016).

Florida Inclusion Network. Retrieved from www.floridainclusionnetwork.com/Uploads/1/docs/centers/CRSRL/FIN/products/CTSessionDTieredLessonPlan Facil.-WebPages4-16-10.pdf

Florida Standards Language Arts Quick Guide. Retrieved from www.fldoe.org/core/fileparse.php/7539/urlt/lafsqrg.pdf

Ford, A., Davern, L., & Schnorr, R. (2001). Learners with significant disabilities: Curricular relevance in an era of standards-based reform. *Remedial and Special Education*, 22(4), 214–222.

Fredricks, J. A., Blumenfeld, P. C., & Paris, A. H. (2004). School engagement: Potential of the concept, state of the evidence. *Review of Educational Research*, 74(1), 59–109.

Goldbart, J., & Ware, J. (2015). Communication. In P. Lacey, H. Lawson, & P. Jones (Eds.), *Educating learners with severe, profound and multiple learning difficulties* (pp. 258–270). London: Routledge.

Gopnik, A., Sobel, D. M., Schulz, L. E., & Glymour, C. (2001). Causal learning mechanisms in very young children: Two-, three-, and four-year-olds infer causal relations from patterns of variation and covariation. *Developmental Psychology*, 37(5), 620–629.

Grove, N., Harwood, J., Henderson, J., Park, K., & Bird, R. (2015). Literature and stories in the lives of learners with SLD/PMLD. In P. Lacey, R. Ashdown, P. Jones, H. Lawson, & M. Pipe (Eds.), *The Routledge companion to severe, profound and multiple learning difficulties* (pp. 305–316). London: Routledge.

Harkins, S. B. (2012). Mainstreaming, the regular education initiative, and inclusion as lived experience, 1974–2004: A practitioner's view. *Inquiry in Education*, (3)1. Retrieved from http://digitalcommons.nl.edu/ie/vol3/iss1/4 (accessed November 18, 2016).

Hentz, S., & Jones, P. (2011). *Collaborate smart*. Washington DC: Council for Exceptional Children.

Ho, A. (2004). To be labelled, or not to be labelled: That is the question. *British Journal of Learning Disabilities*, 32(2), 86–92.

i-Ready Diagnostics. Retrieved from www.curriculumassociates.com (accessed November 18, 2016).

Individuals with Disabilities Education Act (IDEA) of 1997, P.L. 105-17, 20 U.S.C.1400.

Individuals with Disabilities Education Act (IDEA) of 2004, P.L. 108-446, 20 U.S.C.1400.

Iovannone, R., Dunlap, G., Huber, H., & Kincaid, D. (2003). Effective educational practices for students with autism spectrum disorders. *Focus on Autism and Other Developmental Disabilities*, 18, 150–166.

Jacobs, N., & Harvey, D. (2010). The extent to which teacher attitudes and expectations predict academic achievement of final year students. *Educational Studies*, 36(2), 195–206.

Jean Piaget Archives Foundation (1989). *The Jean Piaget Bibliography*. Geneva: Jean Piaget Archives Foundation.

Jones, P., & Gillies, A. (2010). Engaging young children in research about an inclusion project. In R. Rose (Ed.), *Confronting obstacles for inclusion: International responses to developing education* (pp. 123–136). London: Routledge.

Jones, P., & Lawson, H. (2015). Insights into teacher learning about pedagogy from an international group of teachers of pupils with severe intellectual disabilities. *European Journal of Special Education*, (30)3, 384–401.

Jorgensen, C. (2006, August). The least dangerous assumption: A challenge to create a new paradigm. Keynote presentation at the 8th Annual Autism Summer Institute, University of New Hampshire, Durham, New Hampshire.

Lacey, P. (2010). SMART and SCRUFFY targets. *SLD Experience*, 57, 16–21.

Lewis, A., & Norwich, B. (Eds.). (2005). *Special teaching for special children*. Maidenhead: Oxford University Press.

Maag, J. W., Swearer, S. M., & Toland, M. D. (2009). Cognitive-behavioral interventions for depression in children and adolescents: Meta-analysis, promising programs, and implications for school personnel. In M. Mayer, J. Lochman, & R. Van Acker (Eds.), *Cognitive-behavioral interventions for emotional and behavioral disorders: School-based practice* (pp. 235–265). New York: Guilford Press.

Marzano, R. (2001). *Classroom instruction that works: Research-based strategies for increasing student achievement*. VA: ASCD.

Mathematics Florida Standards (MAFS) Structure and Coding. Retrieved from www.cpalms.org/Uploads/docs/FrontMatter/mafs_structure_coding_explanation.pdf

McGregor, G. (2003). Standards-based reform and students with disabilities. In D. L. Ryndak & S. Alper (Eds.), *Curriculum and instruction for students with significant disabilities in inclusive settings* (pp. 31–48). Boston, MA: Pearson Education.

Meyer, L. H., Peck, C., & Brown, L. (1991). *Critical issues in the lives of people with severe disabilities*. Baltimore, MD: Brookes.

National Center and State Collaborative (NCSC) (2015). Retrieved from https://wiki.ncscpartners.org/index.php/Main_Page (accessed November 18, 2016).

No Child Left Behind (NCLB) Act of 2001, Pub. L. No. 107–110, § 115, Stat. 1425 (2002).

Nolet, V., & McLaughlin, M. J. (2005). *Accessing the General Curriculum: Including students with disabilities in standards-based reform*. Thousand Oaks, CA: SAGE.

OASIS, Official Authoritative Site of Multiple IntelligenceS. Retrieved from http://multipleintelligencesoasis.org/ (accessed January 2017).

Parker, M. A., & Schuster, J. W. (2002). Effectiveness of simultaneous prompting on the acquisition of observational and instructive feedback stimuli when teaching a heterogeneous group of high school students. *Education and Training in Mental Retardation and Developmental Disabilities*, 37, 89–104.

Paulsen, G. (1987). *Hatchet*. New York: Simon & Schuster.

Ryndak, D. L., Jackson, L. B., & White, J. M. (2013). Involvement and progress in the general curriculum for students with extensive support needs: K-12 inclusive-education research and implications for the future. *Inclusion*, 1, 28–49.

Schwartz, E., & Davis, A. S. (2006). Reactive attachment disorder: Implications for school readiness and school functioning. *Psychology in the Schools*, 43(4), 471–479.

Silverman, W. K., & Field, A. P. (Eds.). (2011). *Anxiety disorders in children and adolescents*. Cambridge: Cambridge University Press.

Smith, M. K. (2002, 2008). Howard Gardner and multiple intelligences. *The encyclopedia of informal education*. Retrieved from http://infed.org/mobi/howard-gardner-multiple-intelligences-and-education/ (accessed November 18, 2016).

Thompson, S., Thurlow, M., Quenemoen, R., Esler, A., & Whetstone, P. (2001). *Addressing standards and assessments on state IEP forms*. Minneapolis, MN: University of Minnesota, National Center on Educational Outcomes.

Towles-Reeves, E., & Kleinert, H. (2006). The impact of one state's alternate assessment upon instruction and IEP development. *Rural Special Education Quarterly*, 25(3), 31–39.

Turnbull, R., Wehmeyer, M., & Shogren, K. (2010). *Exceptional lives: Special education in today's schools* (6th edn). Columbus, OH: Pearson.

Unique Learning System® Retrieved from https://www.n2y.com (accessed November 18, 2016).

United States Department of Education. "Elementary and Secondary Education Act (ESEA)." 2010.

U.S. Department of Education (2010, March). The reauthorization of ESEA: A blueprint for reform. Retrieved from http://www2.ed.gov/policy/elsec/leg/blueprint/publication_pg7.html (accessed November 18, 2016).

U.S. Department of Education Office of Civil Rights (1995). The civil rights of students with hidden disabilities under Section 504 of the Rehabilitation Act of 1973. Retrieved from http://www2.ed.gov/about/offices/list/ocr/docs/hq5269.html (accessed November 18, 2016).

Uzgiris I. C., & Hunt J. (1975). *Toward ordinal scales of psychological development in infancy*. Champaign, IL: University of Illinois.

Vandereet, J., Maes, B., Lembrechts, D., & Zink, I. (2010). Eliciting proto-imperatives and proto-declaratives in children with intellectual disabilities. *Journal of Applied Research in Intellectual Disabilities*, 23, 154–166.

Ware, J. (1996). *Creating a responsive environment for people with profound and multiple learning difficulties*. London: David Fulton.

Whiten, A., & Erdal, D. (2012). The human socio-cognitive niche and its evolutionary origins. Phil. Trans. Roy. Soc. B 367, 2119–2129.

Wong, C., Odom, S. L., Hume, K. A., Cox, A. W., Fettig, A., Kucharczyk, S., Brock, M. E., Plavnick, J. B., Fleury, V. P., & Schultz, T. R. (2015). Evidence-based practices for children, youth, and young adults with autism spectrum disorder: A comprehensive review. *Journal of Autism and Developmental Disorders*, (7), 1951–1966.

Yell, M. L. (2006). *The law and special education*. Upper Saddle River, NJ: Pearson.

Yell, M. L., Meadows, N. B., Drasgow, E., & Shriner, J. G. (2013). *Evidence based practice for educating students with emotional and behavioral disorders*. Upper Saddle River, NJ: Pearson.

Young, T. (2010). How valid and useful is the notion of learning style? A multicultural investigation. *Procedia Social and Behavioral Sciences*, 2, 427–433.

# Index

Page numbers in *italics* denote tables.